CORDE

The New York, Westchester & Boston Railway

RAILROADS PAST AND PRESENT

George M. Smerk, editor

The New York, Westchester & Boston Railway

J. P. MORGAN'S MAGNIFICENT MISTAKE

HERBERT H. HARWOOD, JR.

Indiana University Press ◉ Bloomington & Indianapolis

This book is a publication of

Indiana University Press
601 North Morton Street
Bloomington, IN 47404-3797 USA

http://iupress.indiana.edu

Telephone orders   800-842-6796
Fax orders   812-855-7931
Orders by e-mail   iuporder@indiana.edu

© 2008 by Herbert H. Harwood, Jr.
All rights reserved

No part of this book may be reproduced or utilized in any form or by any means, electronic or mechanical, including photocopying and recording, or by any information storage and retrieval system, without permission in writing from the publisher. The Association of American University Presses' Resolution on Permissions constitutes the only exception to this prohibition.

The paper used in this publication meets the minimum requirements of American National Standard for Information Sciences—Permanence of Paper for Printed Library Materials, ANSI Z39.48-1984.

Manufactured in the United States of America

Library of Congress Cataloging-in-Publication Data

Harwood, Herbert H.
   The New York, Westchester & Boston Railway : J.P. Morgan's magnificent mistake / Herbert H. Harwood, Jr.
     p. cm
   Includes bibliographical references and index.
   ISBN 978-0-253-35143-2 (cloth : alk. paper) 1. New York, Westchester & Boston Railway—History 2. Railroads—New York (State)—History. 3. Morgan, J. Pierpont (John Pierpont), 1837–1913. I. Title.
   HE2791.N6794H37   2008
385.0974—dc22
                                                         2007039805

1 2 3 4 5 13 12 11 10 09 08

CONTENTS

Acknowledgments ○ *vii*

Introduction: A Railroad Like No Other ○ *1*

1 *Before the Beginning, 1832–1904* ○ *5*

2 *A Deep Fog Descends, 1901–1908* ○ *19*

3 *Building the Perfect Railroad, 1909–1912* ○ *31*

AN NYW&B ARCHITECTURE GALLERY ○ 47

4 *Running the Railroad* ○ *57*

5 *But Why?* ○ *71*

6 *The Phantom Westchester Northern* ○ *79*

7 *Making the Best of Life, 1913–1929* ○ *87*

8 *Down and Out (I): Down, 1930–1936* ○ *105*

9 *Down and Out (II): Out, 1937–1942* ○ *117*

Appendix 1: Roster of Equipment ○ *131*

Appendix 2: NYW&B Station List ○ *135*

Notes ○ *139*

Bibliography ○ *147*

Index ○ *151*

ACKNOWLEDGMENTS

One could say that this book had its genesis 70 years ago when, as a child living in Scarsdale, I would pass over the Westchester tracks at Heathcote on summer trips to Rye Beach with my family. While I never saw a train, I was fascinated by this impressive railroad and its distinctive station at a spot which then seemed to be in the middle of nowhere. The fascination simmered until it popped out again in a rather superficial article done for *Trains* magazine in 1951. That was followed by a 1953 college senior thesis that was dredged out to form the basis for this work.

In writing the thesis, I was able to interview two NYW&B principals who were still living and active then—Alfred Fellheimer, the railroad's original architect, and James L. Dohr, its last receiver. At the time, Mr. Fellheimer was still in architectural practice and Mr. Dohr was a professor of accounting at Columbia University's Graduate School of Business. I was also able to get some valuable insight from Professor Kent Healy at Yale. Professor Healy was a former New Haven officer who ran Yale's graduate program in transportation management. All three gave me priceless help, and they deserve top posthumous honors.

But in my case, making a thesis by a callow 22-year-old into a real book took another 54 years to gain modestly greater maturity, some working railroad experience, better organization, and much more help.

There are a multitude of people who deserve thanks, and, happily, most of them are still living. But the place of honor belongs to Roger Wines, a retired professor of history at Fordham University, who has spent years meticulously researching original documents for a NYW&B book of his own. Not only did he generously share whatever information I needed and answer all questions—saintly acts in themselves—but he slogged through the original manuscript three times, carefully correcting misstatements, adding information, and expunging non sequiturs, unfounded speculations, and grammatical and spelling lapses, as well as clarifying murky descriptions and references. A truly heroic and priceless effort, and this book's final form owes much to his help. May his own work improve on this—which it doubtless will.

Gratitude also goes to Otto Vondrak and Robert A. Bang, two younger Westchester historians who carry the railroad's flame on in books of their own. Otto shared much data that he had uncovered and allowed me to use artwork from another book he had co-authored, and Mr. Bang generously shared photos from his extensive collection, some of which were used in his recent Westchester book.

Michael Weinman, currently a transportation consultant, did a Westchester thesis similar to mine for New York University in 1965, which he copied for me—and more recently he helped me untangle some difficult knots.

Jack W. Swanberg, a career railroad operating officer, New Haven guru, and author of the definitive book *New Haven Power,* helped in several vital ways—not the least of which was providing access to photographs taken between 1911 and 1932 by New Haven electrical engineer Harry F. Brown. Jack also loaned priceless pieces from his bottomless New Haven collection, answered questions as only someone experienced in New Haven railroad operations can, and helped provide leads to more material.

Bernard Linder, a New York City traction historian, was invaluable in shedding light on the confused history of NYW&B bus operations. The late Roger Arcara, who published the first formal book on the Westchester, *Westchester's Forgotten Railway,* was, needless to say, a fountain of knowledge as well as an intelligent and bountiful correspondent. Roger should also be commended for reproducing various key trade magazine articles describing the Westchester's original construction and equipment that now are highly scarce in their original form.

Other help came from Gregory P. Ames, Curator of the John W. Barriger III National Railroad Library in St. Louis; Andy Bass; Donald Engel; George W. Harwood; LeRoy O. King, Jr.; Steven Meyers; Steve J. Pappas; John Stern; and J. William Vigrass. And thanks, too, to Marjorie Noll for her inspired design work, and Elise Meyer-Bothling for her meticulous indexing.

And then there are the photos. Here particular thanks go to Alfred Seibel, who decades ago provided me with many of his prints, and, more recently, Dave Keller—who made prints from many of George Votava's photos now in his collection—and Bob Liljestrand, of Bob's Photo, who also has some of Votava's photos which he sells.

And finally, there was the job of making the thing into a book, and, indeed, deciding whether it should be a book at all. For all that, thanks go to the folks at Indiana University Press—most particularly my editor, Linda Oblack, who decided that, yes, it should be a book and pushed it through; the copyeditor, Elaine Otto, who helped make it readable; the managing editor, Miki Bird, who shepherded it through production; and the book designer, Jamison Cockerham, who created the jacket and interior design.

The New York, Westchester & Boston Railway

The New York, Westchester & Boston at its fullest development c. 1930. © Otto M. Vondrak.

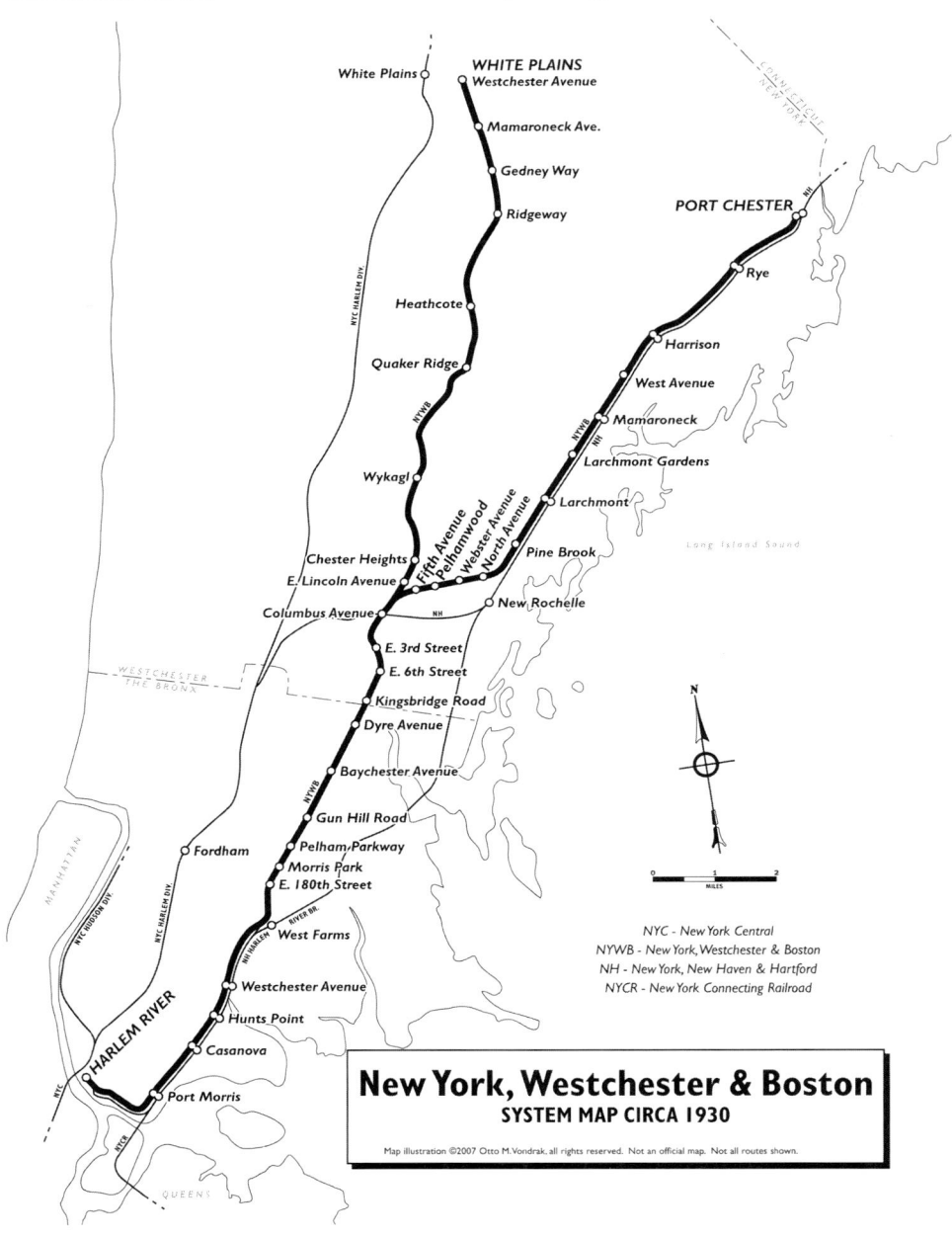

x ◉ The New York, Westchester & Boston Railway

INTRODUCTION: A RAILROAD LIKE NO OTHER

It was at once beautiful and bizarre. When the New York, Westchester & Boston Railway opened in 1912, it was one of the engineering wonders of the American railroad world—the finest, most advanced, and most expensive of its type anywhere. As the professional journals of the time proclaimed, it was also a bold statement of foresight and faith in the future. And behind it—unbeknownst to almost everyone—was none other than the reigning financial power of his time, J. Pierpont Morgan.

Built to the highest engineering standards and operated with strict punctuality, the Westchester was a high-speed, high-capacity electric line designed to develop and serve upper-income communities in one of New York City's most rapidly growing suburban areas. It was also one of the strangest projects in American railroad history. Its genesis is shrouded in mysterious and sometimes sordid political and financial dealings that even today remain opaque.

The motivations of its builders are equally indecipherable. Here was a railroad built for what was then a breathtaking $1.2 million per mile simply to construct and equip—almost $24 million a mile in 2005 dollars. But that was not the only cost. Mysterious, unrecorded millions, paid out for unknown reasons even before property was bought and construction began, raised the total to over $2 million a mile, or about $40 million by 2005 values. Yet this railroad, designed to carry more than 100,000 people a day efficiently and comfortably, either ran through virtually undeveloped territory or exactly duplicated the line of the parent company that built it.

Then there was another paradox: This superb piece of design, construction, and operation had one of the most woeful financial performances on record. It never came close to showing a profit. Not once did it show a deficit of less than $1 million—mile for mile the worst anywhere in the railroad industry.

Financial performance was not all. The Westchester was built and owned by the New York, New Haven & Hartford Railroad, at the time one of the country's richest and most respected railroads—and the pride of J. P. Morgan, who dominated its board and handpicked its president. Thanks in part to the Westchester and the dealings behind its creation, the New Haven was brought to near-financial ruin and the indignity of several state and federal investigations that revealed profligate waste, corruption, and mismanagement in its affairs. The near-ruin of 1913 eventually turned to outright bankruptcy in 1935, with the Westchester still providing one of the heavy millstones tied around the New Haven's neck.

And in the end, it all came to nothing. Within 25 years of their start, Westchester trains had stopped running. Five years later, after futile attempts to save it by the communities that it had nurtured, all of the railroad but four miles in the Bronx was dismantled and transformed into World War II scrap. In all, its last years were a depressing case example of multiple shortsightedness ending in an irretrievable loss. Today, it is scarcely remembered—little more than scattered and mostly unnoticed remnants in a prosperous county that could well use it.

But it had quite a life.

Then, as now, railroading in central Westchester County was dominated by the New York & Harlem and its successors. This lithe specimen, NY&H No. 6, is ready to take its train out of Grand Central Depot, probably in the 1870s. It was turned out by Rogers in 1852. Author's collection.

1
BEFORE THE BEGINNING, 1832–1904

By late summer of 1912, all was ready. In less than three years, engineers and contractors had blasted, filled, erected long, heavy steel viaducts and 66 other steel and concrete bridges, built a 4,000-foot-long tunnel, installed a complex electrification with sophisticated signaling and communications systems, built aesthetically distinctive stations, and otherwise created a heavy-duty, state-of-the-art passenger railway.

The New York, Westchester & Boston Railway was an odd but impressive venture, built into a territory that was poised for explosive growth. Westchester County lay just north of New York City. In the nineteenth century it was a woodsy, rural area of rolling hills, devoted mostly to small farms, country summer estates, and water-powered mills on modest rivers such as the Bronx, Hutchinson, and Saw Mill. Bordering the Bronx on its south (and once encompassing parts of that borough), the Hudson River to its east and Long Island Sound and Connecticut on the west, Westchester offered an almost idyllic locale for upper-class suburban development. The countryside was pleasant, pretty, and unspoiled; the Sound's beaches were nearby, and it could boast the best direct transportation into the city. And while it is difficult to imagine now, the northeastern section of the Bronx was semirural and relatively unpopulated. If it lacked some of Westchester's charms, it was nonetheless also a prime area for suburban development.

Already on hand were four established rail lines, including one of America's earliest—the New York & Harlaem Rail-Road. On November 26, 1832, New York City—then huddled at the lower end of Manhattan—witnessed the beginning of a new era when horse-drawn NY&H cars began grinding over strap iron rails from Prince Street to 14th Street at Union Square. From there the company planned to build north along the line of then-nonexistent Fourth Avenue to the Harlem River at 129th Street. Basically the NY&H was to be little more than an unpretentious urban horsecar line, the first and only one of its kind for many years afterward.

Its route through hilly and rocky upper Manhattan was anything but easy, and reaching the river took five years. A deep rock cut had to be blasted through Murray Hill (later roofed over to be a tunnel, and still in existence), a genuine tunnel at Mount Prospect between 92nd and 94th Streets, a wood trestle over the marshy "Harlem Flats," and another cut at "Snake Hill." NY&H horsecars finally reached the Harlem River in October 1837.

But less than a year later, the Harlaem, as it was called (soon simplified to Harlem), decided on a more grandiose goal: it would proceed northward to create an all-rail route to Albany. There it would link with a chain of railroads and the Erie Canal to form a continuous route to the Great Lakes at Buffalo.

At the time, Hudson River steamboats reigned supreme in the New York–Albany trade, and the Harlem's cautious promoters preferred to avoid legal and political problems with their owners. So rather than build along the virtually gradeless east bank of the Hudson, they elected an inland route through the center of Westchester County and the hilly country to its north.

Harlem tracks started northward again in 1840, crossing the Harlem River and heading through what is now the central Bronx (then Westchester County), passing Morrisania and Fordham, and reaching William's Bridge near the present Bronx–Westchester line on September 3, 1842. Following the Bronx River valley, the New York & Harlem pushed on through the village of Tuckahoe, the hamlet of Underhill's Crossing (now Bronxville), and the town of Scarsdale. Finally, on December 1, 1844, its little single-driver steam locomotives chuffed into the county seat village of White Plains, 26 miles from City Hall.

Here the Harlem paused for a while, contemplating the more rugged terrain ahead and dredging up more money to build through it. It was not until January 10, 1852, that its first train entered Chatham Four Corners, New York, 130 miles from New York City and the Harlem's final terminal. At Chatham it connected with the Western Railroad of Massachusetts, which continued west to Albany.[1] Meanwhile, as a testament to the railroad's influence and power, the availability of reliable train service shifted the center of gravity of some Westchester communities. The nexus of both Tuckahoe and Scarsdale, for instance, moved over half a mile east from the colonial era White Plains Post Road to the Harlem tracks along the Bronx River. In Scarsdale's case, what had been Popham's Gate flag stop became the location of the post office and stores that followed.

While the Harlem's builders were struggling through the hills north of White Plains, the New York & New Haven was heading west from New Haven along the Long Island Sound shoreline toward the city. By 1846 it had reached the New York–Connecticut state line and had begun negotiating with the Harlem to use its New York City terminals. Financially needy after its expensive construction in Manhattan and its northward slog through White Plains, the Harlem was all too happy to accommodate. The two parties signed an agreement in March 1848, allowing the New York & New Haven to use Harlem tracks from Woodlawn (at the present north end of the Bronx) to Canal Street in the city.[2] The NY&NH also did its part to affect Westchester communities; before it came through, Mount Vernon did not exist as such.

Sadly for the Harlem, however, its dream of forming a trunk line to Albany and the west had already faded. Thanks in part to its own role in proving rail travel safe, fast, and comfortable, it helped hasten its own doom. The Hudson River Railroad, organized in 1846, succeeded in beating down steamboat opposition and completed its direct, gradeless right-of-way along the Hudson to Albany in 1851. Robbed of its through traffic before it even had a chance, the Harlem quickly succumbed to bankruptcy and permanent status as a local railroad. It did have one huge strategic asset, though—its entry into New York City's commercial and residential core.

Then came the Commodore. One of New York's most successful steamboat operators was Cornelius Vanderbilt of Staten Island. Rough-hewn and tobacco-spitting he may have been, but "Commodore" Vanderbilt was wily and perceptive, and although he was in his 60s, he saw the future and plunged into it. Starting with the New York & Harlem, he executed a spectacular series of financial coups, gathering in the Hudson River Railroad and the original New York Central. Now owning a through route between New York and the Great Lakes at Buffalo, he began maneuvering westward toward Chicago. In 1869 he consolidated his eastern conquests as the New York Central & Hudson River Railroad, and he eventually came to control one of the East's largest and most powerful rail systems.[3]

Vanderbilt's expanding empire was built on the base of the Hudson River Railroad, and he had little interest in the hapless Harlem—except for that New York City entryway. He promptly connected his Hudson River line with the Harlem in the south Bronx, and in 1871 he completed his grandiose Grand Central Depot on its line at 42nd Street and Fourth (now Park) Avenue. Grand Central served the entire Vanderbilt system as well as the New Haven, which remained a tenant in what amounted to perpetuity. (As is well known, 23rd Street marked the city's practical upper limit at that time, and passengers used New York & Harlem horsecars to travel to and from the new terminal.)

Otherwise, what was now the New York Central's Harlem Division was left to its rural ways. But even then, its direct access to the city was encouraging people to escape the crowding, high rents, and smells for Westchester's leafy hills. (And the city smells were memorable, as all local transportation was animal-powered.) The first recognition of this new "commuter" business had come in 1853, when the then-independent Harlem advertised special low rates for daily suburban travel. Among the first commuters was newspaper publisher Horace Greeley, who rode every day between his home in Chappaqua, north of White Plains, and his office in New York. The New Haven also began to enjoy an increasingly brisk business. As early as the end of the Civil War, it was carrying 129

This was Westchester County in the late 1880s. Seemingly in no hurry to go anywhere, New York Central & Hudson River No. 623, an 1880 Schenectady product, sits idly in pastoral surroundings somewhere on the Harlem Division. Author's collection.

Before the Beginning • 7

commuters from Mount Vernon (newly created in 1851), 97 from New Rochelle, 44 from Mamaroneck, 32 from Rye, and 36 from Port Chester.[4] By this time, too, the old New York & New Haven had done its own consolidating and expanding, emerging in 1872 as the New York, New Haven & Hartford and eventually controlling most of southern New England's railroad network.

Following the Civil War, the railroad came into its own as the primary means of land transportation. The technology matured quickly and rail transportation was beginning to change the form of industries and communities. Suddenly railroads were being proposed and built everywhere, and large trunk line systems such as the New York Central were forming and warring with one another for new markets. Some of the new railroad projects were sound and essential, some represented sincere but misplaced hopes of ambitious communities, and some were simply schemes to make money from security sales or construction contracts. Some, too, were outright commercial blackmail, designed to encroach on some established railroad's territory and be bought out. Whatever their promoters' motives, many ended up as phantoms, appearing and disappearing with little or no real work done.

Because of its strategic position as New York City's only land gateway to New England, Westchester County saw a goodly number of these dreams come and go. Would-be builders were especially eager to enter the New York–Boston market. Although the evolving New Haven system had already taken the best routes and markets along the Long Island Sound shore and the Connecticut River—and had its priceless entry to Grand Central—its dominance did not discourage others from trying to invade its markets.

The only one to fully materialize, though, was the ill-starred New York City & Northern, completed in 1881 as the hoped-for New York connection for a competing "inland route" to Boston. The NYC&N started inauspiciously at the Ninth Avenue elevated's terminal at 155th Street and Eighth Avenue in upper Manhattan, twisted its way up the Saw Mill River valley and Pocantico Hills, and ended 53 miles north at Brewster, New York. At Brewster (which was also a station on the Harlem), the NYC&N connected with the New York & New England Railroad, which was doing its best to become a serious New Haven rival for the Hartford and Boston business. Poverty-stricken from the start, the NYC&N bounced from bankruptcy to bankruptcy as a pawn of the New York & New England and others seeking a route into New York. In 1894, at the behest of J. P. Morgan and the New Haven, the New York Central took it off the market and neutralized the threat. As the Central's Putnam Division, it became pretty much a living footnote in the area's railroad history—a charming, bucolic, off-the-beaten path, single-track branch line, nestled in its own nineteenth-century world in an otherwise vibrant and populous Westchester County.[5]

Another such scheme was the Harlem River & Port Chester Railroad, which presented a more direct and serious threat to the New Haven. In 1867 this company projected a line from the Harlem River in the Bronx (then Westchester County) to Port Chester, New York, paralleling the New Haven's mainline much of the way. It was also poised to get a Connecticut charter and, presumably, keep going east alongside its rival. The New Haven soon succumbed to the apparent blackmail and leased the unbuilt railroad two years later. But despite its dubious designs, the Harlem River & Port Chester did have some value. The New Haven used its charter to build a branch south from its mainline at New Rochelle to the Harlem River at 132nd Street and Willis Avenue in the Bronx. Completed in 1873, the Harlem River Branch became the New Haven's freight gateway to New York Harbor, handling shipments that were floated to and from all railroads entering New York, as well as ocean ships and local industries around the harbor. After 1917, the line became even more important as the northern end of the Hell Gate Bridge route between New York and New England.[6]

Then there were various wispy projects that never got beyond the planning or fund-raising stages and deservedly dropped into oblivion. One, though, needs our attention. On March 20, 1872, a company called the New York, Westchester & Boston Railroad obtained a New York charter to build from the Harlem River to Port Chester. This was an odd coincidence, since the New Haven had recently paid to stifle a similar project. This particular company also planned a branch running north to White Plains and then west to Elmsford, as well as a short branch from East 177th Street in the Bronx to Clason's Point and Throg's Neck, in an almost-unpopulated area of what is now the far eastern Bronx bordering on Long Island Sound.[7] Like the Harlem River & Port Chester, all of the NYW&B's proposed route lay in Westchester County, as it was at that time.

If the company's name were taken seriously, it seemed to be yet another scheme to reach into New England and possibly more blackmail for the New Haven. But that question turned out to be academic; after its promoters had spent some $200,000 in acquiring franchises and real estate and beginning some construction, the company collapsed in the 1873 financial panic and subsequent depression. Three years after its inception, a receiver was appointed and the New York, Westchester & Boston disappeared into limbo with nothing more accomplished—dormant, but not dead.[8]

By the turn of the twentieth century, the competitive threats had either died on their own or been directly quashed. Under the aegis of J. P. Morgan (who served on both boards), the New York Central and New Haven stayed mostly in harmony and worked cooperatively to keep peace in the New York and New England territory.

Peace was achieved, at least as far as railroad rivalries were concerned. But much else had been happening in the late nineteenth century that would affect the two railroads' operations and traffic in the New York area. Upper Manhattan and the Bronx underwent a profound change as steam-powered elevated railways were built up the length of narrow Manhattan island, bringing fast, cheap transportation to the scattered little villages and farmlands. By 1880, four elevated trunk lines reached from one end of the island to the other, and as the "els" moved north, so did the city's population.

The Bronx came next. In 1886 the Suburban Rapid Transit Company opened the first el line across the Harlem River. The Suburban was, in effect, an extension of the Manhattan Railway's Second and Third Avenue el routes; beginning at 129th Street in Manhattan, it first terminated at 143rd Street in the Bronx, but by 1902 it reached as far north as Fordham University and Bronx Park. By coincidence, it passed close to the New Haven's Harlem River Branch terminal at 132nd Street by the river, and a spur was built to join the two lines there. Between 1891 and 1905 the New Haven used it to operate a busy through suburban service between New Rochelle and the 129th Street elevated terminal, serving Pelham Manor and such then-isolated Bronx communities as Baychester, Port Morris, West Farms, and Hunt's Point. As many as 40 trains a day shuttled over this route, made up of short, elevated-style coaches hauled behind small Forney-design steam locomotives. (Although the direct service to upper Manhattan ended in 1905, the New Haven continued what it called its "suburban line" service to the Harlem River, where passengers transferred to an elevated shuttle, and when it rebuilt the Harlem River Branch in the early 1900s, it also constructed many elaborate masonry stations for its use.)[9]

Electrification comes to Manhattan's "els." A train of 1907-vintage IRT rolling stock negotiates the "S" curve at Coenties Slip on the Second Avenue elevated in 1940. Author's collection.

In the last years of Grand Central steam operations, 16 New York Central 2-6-6T tank engines like this shuttled suburban trains on the Harlem and Hudson lines. No. 1411, probably at North White Plains, had a short life in such service. Built in 1902, it was rebuilt to a conventional 2-6-0 in 1906. Author's collection.

While all this was happening, electricity came to urban rapid transit and suburban rail operations, making them faster, cleaner, and cheaper to run. In 1888 the electrical engineer Frank J. Sprague demonstrated a practical method of street railway electrification and spawned a massive proliferation of trolley lines. Following up on that, Sprague developed what was called multiple-unit control, which allowed a single motorman to operate an entire train of electrically powered cars. Multiple unit control—or simply "m.u." as the trade abbreviated it—made possible electrification of the elevated lines and steam-powered railroad suburban services, as well as the construction of subways. Sprague successfully demonstrated the system in Chicago in 1897; by the next year, one Chicago elevated line had converted to electricity, and the Brooklyn el system had begun. The Manhattan Railway held out briefly, but had fully electrified its elevated system by 1903.[10] New York also wasted no time building its first subway, which opened in 1904 and included a branch into the Bronx as far north as 180th Street and Bronx Park, the borough's second rapid transit line.

Nor were electricity's implications lost on the New York Central and New Haven, who were struggling to cope with ever-increasing congestion on their lines into Grand Central, all of which funneled into a long tunnel under Park Avenue. The Commodore's old Grand Central Depot had been substantially remodeled between 1899 and 1901 and renamed Grand Central Station, but a new façade and interior layout did nothing to help the smoky mess behind.[11]

The Central had been studying electrification of its terminal zone since 1899, and the New Haven was also experimenting with electric traction on some branch lines. But in 1902 a horrific wreck in the smoke-filled Park Avenue tunnel brought things swiftly to a head. New York State passed a law prohibiting steam power in Manhattan after mid-1908, and both railroads hastened to comply. Planning only to electrify its terminal and Westchester County suburban zones, the Central adopted the already proven 600-volt direct current third-rail system used by the subway and elevated lines. The more ambitious New Haven intended to extend its electric operations at least to New Haven, Connecticut, and ultimately Boston. George Westinghouse thus seduced the railroad with his newly developed and revolutionary 11,000-volt single-phase alternating current system, delivered from overhead wires, which allowed cheaper long-distance current transmission than the lower-voltage DC. But since New Haven trains used New York Central tracks into Grand Central, their locomotives and later multiple-unit cars had to operate on both systems, making a nonstop changeover at the Woodlawn junction.

The Central ran its ceremonial inaugural electric train from Grand Central to High Bridge in the Bronx on September 30, 1906. The New Haven followed on July 24, 1907, running only to New Rochelle, but by October the wires were energized and trains were running to Stamford, Connecticut, the end of the railroad's commuter zone. (In the beginning the Central's electrification extended only to High Bridge on its Hudson Division and Wakefield, near Mount Vernon, on the Harlem. It was not until 1910 that the Harlem electrification was completed to North White Plains, and 1913 to Croton-on-Hudson.) Electrification also allowed the long-overdue replacement of Grand Central with today's magnificent Grand Central Terminal, begun in 1903 and completed 11 years later.[12]

Even before the two railroads electrified, they had embarked on substantial rebuilding projects aimed at increasing capacity, eliminating grade crossings, and providing more suitable suburban facilities for the growing number of better-to-do suburban passengers. For its Harlem Division, the Central built four tracks without grade crossings on

Beginning in 1906, the newly electrified "steam" railroads also did their part to develop the Bronx and lower Westchester County. Here a typical set of original New York Central m.u. cars pauses at Tremont station on the four-track section of the Harlem Division shared with New Haven trains. Walter Broschart photo, author's collection.

the busy section shared with the New Haven to Woodlawn, and double-tracked the line north of there. During the 1890s the New Haven had four-tracked its mainline and also eliminated all grade crossings. At the same time, attractive architect-designed stations began to appear to replace the simple wood "country depots" of the post–Civil War era. Scarsdale, for example, received a handsome Tudor-style station in 1902 that, at the time, seemed a bit overstated for a town of about 900 people loosely spread over 6.6 square miles. (It still served 20 times that population in 2007.)

Spurred by new rapid transit lines and improved railroad service, the Bronx and lower Westchester County began growing rapidly. The Bronx's population more than doubled between 1900 and 1910 as it became a haven for middle-class families living in apartment houses. By 1910, 431,000 people were living there. While the gross numbers were much smaller, the Westchester communities were showing some of the same relative increases. Overall, population in Westchester's central and eastern sections grew by two-thirds, and many individual communities did much better. Along the Sound shore, New Rochelle, Pelham, Harrison, and Mamaroneck showed population increases ranging from 73 percent to over 100 percent. Inland, White Plains and Eastchester both more than doubled. Admittedly, the actual population numbers were still modest. Still showing the vestiges of a rural county seat, the village of White Plains had 16,000 residents in 1910, and genuinely bucolic Eastchester, to its south, had only 6,400. But the municipalities at the county's southern end were developing into genuine small cities.

Although shot in 1951, this scene typifies suburban operations on the New York Central's Harlem Division after electrification. The view looks south at the junction with the New Haven at Woodlawn. Author's photo.

Mount Vernon, bordering the Bronx in the county's central section, was now up to 31,000, and New Rochelle, along the Sound, was close behind at 29,000.[13]

It was into this environment that the New York, Westchester & Boston emerged Venus-like in 1912, fully grown and, by railroad standards, just as gorgeous. But while the railroad was a dazzling showpiece, its back story was something else—a strange, complicated tale of aborted dreams, dubious motives, covert and mysterious financial dealings, and, in the end, a wildly extravagant enterprise that seemed to have no purpose.

As noted already, the New York, Westchester & Boston story dated back to the early 1870s. But it really began shortly after the turn of the twentieth century with the intersection of Westchester County's blossoming suburban development and two ruling institutions of the time, J. Pierpont Morgan and the New York, New Haven & Hartford Railroad.

At a time when railroads were the dominant form of transportation, the New Haven had heavily populated southern New England virtually to itself. Its constantly busy mainline connected New York's Grand Central with Providence and Boston, and major branches reached north to Hartford and Springfield, Worcester, Fitchburg, and Pittsfield, Massachusetts. In between was a dense thicket of branches serving virtually every population center of note in Connecticut, Rhode Island, and southeastern Massachusetts. Through passenger trains using its lines reached Montreal, Portland and Bangor, Maine, and Washington, D.C. Heavily traveled New Haven suburban trains operated northeast from New York and south and southeast from Boston. Vacationers rode special excursions to Cape Cod, Maine, the Berkshires, and White Mountains. And needless to say, southern New England mills and manufacturers—then thriving in an era before cheap southern labor—lived by New Haven freight services, as did consumers of coal (then universal for home heating), food, building materials, and anything else brought in from the outside.

The New Haven also was a solid financial rock. By railroad standards, its debt ratio was low, and both Wall Street and the conservative New England banks considered its stock gold-plated, selling at $200 a share or more by 1903.[14] Perhaps as a gesture of self-congratulation the railroad even named one of its premier New York–Boston trains the "Gilt Edge Limited."

If it could be said that J. P. Morgan had any railroad sentiment, it was for the New Haven Railroad. Born in Hartford, he had ridden its trains from boyhood. Among his numerous other involvements, he had been a director of the New York, Providence & Boston Railroad since 1887. When the New Haven absorbed it in 1892, Morgan moved over to its board, joining ally William Rockefeller there.[15] Afterward, the New Haven was "his" railroad. Far from being a nominal board member, he immediately made it his personal fiefdom, and his fellow directors became meek, albeit well-heeled, serfs.

Morgan had made his reputation by controlling what had been wasteful, capital-consuming competition in the railroad industry. While reluctantly acknowledging the necessity of competition, he abhorred the free-for-all empire-building battles that were reducing investment returns and jeopardizing security values. Scarcely had he arrived at the New Haven than he brutally destroyed the ambitions of A. A. McLeod, the overly ambitious president of the Philadelphia & Reading Railroad and a typical example of the sort of reckless entrepreneur that Morgan despised. McLeod had boldly invaded New England by taking control of the Boston & Maine Railroad, a prime New Haven connection to the north and a New England trunk line in its own right, as well as the New York & New England, a direct New Haven competitor.

With McLeod gone and the New York & New England and other lines taken into the New Haven fold, Morgan looked at other modes of competition. While his New Haven surely dominated its territory, he was bothered by competition from the Long Island Sound steamship lines and the rapidly expanding network of electric street railways, not to mention the constant implied threats of new railroad schemes in this lucrative market. (In retrospect, the trolley lines were really doing the New Haven a favor by helping to siphon off its barely profitable local passenger business.)

Determined to put all of southern New England under a New Haven–ruled *Pax Morganiana*, in 1903 Morgan recruited his protégé, Charles S. Mellen, then president of the Northern Pacific, to come east and run the company to his specifications. A native New Englander himself (from Lowell, Massachusetts), the bright, capable Mellen had worked his way up the railroad management ladder, and by 1892 he was general manager of McLeod's New York & New England. As he told it, the New Haven bought him off by making him its vice president in charge of traffic. It was in that job that he antagonized the New York Central, another major Morgan interest, and thus aroused Morgan himself. In a rare personal confrontation with The Presence, he won his case—and Morgan's grudging respect. In 1896, Morgan had finished reorganizing the Northern Pacific in collaboration with the Great Northern's James J. Hill, the NP's chief competitor. Subsequently the NP and GN were meant to be more cooperative neighbors, under the "friendly" guidance of Jim Hill. Morgan picked Mellen as the NP's president, but when Mellen proved too eager to build up his railroad at the Great Northern's

J. P. Morgan graphically demonstrates why few people cared to argue with him, including any New Haven directors. The photo dates to about 1902, when he ruled the New Haven along with numerous other enterprises. Library of Congress, negative LC-USZ62-8681.

Charles S. Mellen displays a shining pate and haughty air in this c. 1902 photo, taken when he assumed the New Haven presidency. Jack W. Swanberg collection.

expense, he and Hill became anything but happy partners. When Morgan called him in 1903 to come to New Haven, he happily accepted.[16]

By then the aging Morgan (he was 66 in 1903) was preoccupied with a multitude of other things, both business and his art and manuscript acquisitions. As he did with other trusted lieutenants, he charged Mellen with the job of pacifying the New Haven's territory by buying out what was left of the rail competition as well as those irritating steamship and trolley lines. "A glacially bald man, soft-voiced, reputedly cold in his official dealings," Mellen was also aggressive, articulate, and imaginative.[17]

Furthermore, his energy and expansionist nature fitted him nicely for Morgan's goals. Morgan was known to hate haggling over price, effectively giving Mellen a blank check. Taking it, he enthusiastically began a wholesale assault, buying up all the railroad, steamship, and streetcar companies he could lay his hands on—often at absurdly inflated prices. In 1904 the New Haven absorbed the Central New England Railroad, another McLeod orphan and the last independent line in southern New England. (While much of the CNE was left to wither, its mainline gave the New Haven a highly strategic and valuable freight gateway to Pennsylvania and the west via a bridge over the Hudson River at Poughkeepsie, New York.) By devious, extralegal means, Mellen also bought control of the Boston & Maine. By 1910 or so he had finished the job. Nearly every important trolley company in Connecticut and Rhode Island was under New Haven control, as well as Massachusetts systems in Worcester, Springfield, and the Berkshires region—and all the steamship companies. In short, almost everything that moved in southern New England was a New Haven vassal in one form or another.

These adventures eventually brought on disaster and more, but that is getting ahead of the story. Here let it just be noted that business and transportation historians continue a never-to-be-resolved controversy over who was most responsible for this wild acquisition spree and the subsequent collapse—Morgan or Mellen. Some Morgan biographers maintain that Mellen ran rampant behind his unknowing boss's back, while—as will be seen later—Mellen himself claimed he was merely following orders. In fact, both shared abundant blame.[18]

During Mellen's buying orgy, one perceived competitive threat appeared at the west end of the New Haven's territory. Actually, it was two threats in one. A pair of rival railroad promotions proposed to poach on the New Haven's New York suburban zone by building what were advertised as high-speed rapid transit–type electric lines between New York and Westchester County, both of them paralleling the New Haven's Harlem River Branch and its mainline (as well as each other) between the Bronx and Port Chester, New York. The two had materialized shortly after the turn of the twentieth century—one in 1901 and the other three years later—and planned to exploit southern Westchester's dawning suburban boom. Nobody now knows the promoters' real motives. Perhaps one or both genuinely believed that a modern electric service, connected to the city's elevateds and subway, would be a greater stimulant to real estate development and would generate more railroad passenger business than could the existing railroads. Or perhaps they just saw money to be made from construction contracts which, in their case, could be quite lucrative. Or maybe one or both were classic blackmailers, with buy-anything Mellen and the New Haven as the prime marks.

Whatever their aims, what they accomplished was something very different—a legal, political, and financial morass involving influential bankers, troubled banks, the Panic of 1907, and ultimately J. P. Morgan and Charles S. Mellen.

The New York & Port Chester, as originally planned in 1901. From *Electric Railway Journal* 18 (1901): 81, author's collection.

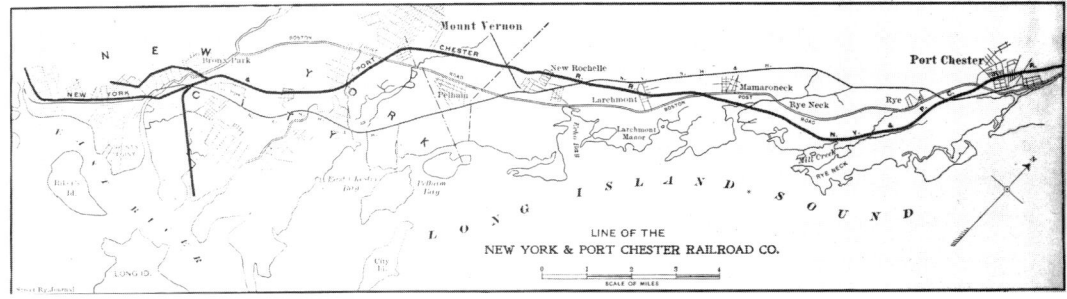

2
A DEEP FOG DESCENDS, 1901–1908

As electricity revolutionized the economics and reach of city transit, it quickly inspired entrepreneurs and investors to apply the technology to reach communities beyond the urban areas that were inadequately served or neglected by the steam railroads. In the early 1900s, millions of dollars were poured into building electric "interurbans," which essentially used street railway technology adapted for higher speeds and longer distances. Such investments, sadly, vaporized as cheap automobiles and paved roads appeared. But a few other entrepreneurs were more prescient and saw opportunities for more elaborate quasi-rapid transit lines that could open undeveloped suburban real estate.

One was electrical engineer William C. Gotshall. A St. Louis native and Lehigh University graduate, Gotshall had first worked in research and development for the Missouri Electric Light and Power Company, then graduated to building electric railway lines in Missouri, Illinois, Indiana, and Louisiana. In 1897 he came to New York to electrify the Second Avenue Railway's horsecar operations. There he got the idea of promoting an electric rapid transit–style railroad into Westchester. At the time, New York Central and New Haven suburban trains still consisted of wooden coaches hauled by soot-spewing steam engines into an overcrowded, obsolete Grand Central. His apparent reasoning was that clean, modern electric cars, perhaps entering the city via the elevated lines or proposed subway, would attract commuters and build suburban communities where little so far existed.

Gathering a group of backers, Gotshall incorporated the New York & Port Chester Railroad on April 5, 1901.[1] His NY&PC was to build a four-track, third-rail electric railroad from New York City to Port Chester, New York, serving the eastern Bronx, New Rochelle, Larchmont, and Mamaroneck along the way. Basically the route would follow the abortive New York, Westchester & Boston scheme of the early 1870s, including a branch to Clason's Point in the eastern Bronx, but omitting the old company's branch to White Plains and Elmsford. The Port Chester road's southern terminal was to be on the Harlem River at 132nd Street in the Bronx, where it would connect with the Third Avenue Elevated. Another branch would reach a second terminal at 177th Street in the West Farms area of the Bronx, where it would join an extension of the to-be-built city subway line. Using either or both of these connections, NY&PC trains could be run directly into Manhattan, giving passengers a wide choice of city destinations.

Elaborate plans and schedules were worked out: The railroad was to be laid with 90-pound rail, the heaviest then in general use. It would have no grade crossings and would employ 85 modern concrete bridges to cross all roadways and other railroads. Local and express trains would run at speeds of 60 mph and more.[2]

Reputedly behind Gotshall were two of Morgan's nemeses, the flamboyant, free-wheeling financier Charles W. Morse and his friend John W. "Bet-a-Million" Gates, who had organized a contracting company called the New York Railroad & Development Company to build it.[3] Although the details of his financing seemed uncertain, and apparently there were no firm interchange agreements between his railroad and the city rapid transit companies, Gotshall managed to have the NY&PC well publicized, and communities along the route enthusiastically supported it. The New York Railroad Commission granted the company permission to build on April 9, 1902.[4]

Clearly, Gotshall's new railroad almost precisely paralleled the New Haven's mainline and Harlem River Branch its entire route, except for the Clason's Point Branch and the short spur to the projected subway at 177th Street. To nobody's surprise, lawyers from the railroad and its trolley subsidiary, the New York & Stamford Railway, descended, making the obvious argument that the New York & Port Chester was unnecessary since the territory already was well served by the two companies.[5]

What *did* surprise, though, was the appearance, or rather reappearance, of a rival group that proposed a virtually identical suburban electric line between New York and Port Chester. Injunctions began to fly, and Gotshall's ambitious project ground to a halt before any significant construction had begun.

In 1900 these new promoters had tried to organize a railway into the county under the name of the New York City & Westchester, but found that their charter was invalid. Looking around for an alternate corporate vehicle, someone dug up the 1872 New York, Westchester & Boston, whose corporate shell and charter its dedicated and diligent receiver had managed to keep alive through a 28-year hibernation. On December 23, 1903, the first steps were taken to bring the old enterprise out of receivership, and new articles of association were filed January 6, 1904. Capitalization was set at $20 million in stock and $20 million in bonds, $15 million of which was to be issued immediately and $5 million held for future expansion. As seemed to be usual, this group also organized its own construction company, the City & County Contract Company, as well as the New York & Westchester Townsite Company—apparently a real estate development enterprise. Less is known about who they were, or why they were essentially playing a spoiler role against Gotshall, but the list of officers and directors seemed to indicate money and stability (and, by later evidence, Tammany Hall connections).

William Lanman Bull, a New York banker associated with Edward Sweet & Company and formerly president of the New York Stock Exchange, served as president. Samuel Hunt of Cincinnati, the capable president of the anemic Detroit Southern Railway (which he helped reorganize as the Detroit, Toledo & Ironton), was listed as vice president. (Sadly, Hunt was a short-timer; he died in May 1905.) There appeared to be some sort of association with the Interborough Rapid Transit, which by 1904 not only was completing the new subway but controlled all of the elevated lines in Manhattan and the Bronx. William Barclay Parsons, the legendary chief engineer of the subway project, was listed as both a consulting engineer and company director, while another NYW&B director, Andrew Freedman, served on the executive committee of both the IRT and its

The planned routes of the New York, Westchester & Boston, as it was revived in 1904. The Throg's Neck Branch is at the lower right, but in this map the original company's line between White Plains and Elmsford seemingly has been discarded. Other heavy lines shown in the Bronx are elevated and subway routes. Following New Haven control, much of the NYW&B route was revised, and the Throg's Neck Branch was dropped. From NYW&B Ry. prospectus, 1905, author's collection.

associated Rapid Transit Subway Construction Company. The railroad also put together a line engineering staff headed by William A. Pratt, recently a division engineer on the Baltimore & Ohio.[6]

Like the New York & Port Chester, the resuscitated NYW&B planned a four-track electric line from the Harlem River to Port Chester with a branch to the new subway station at East 177th Street in the Bronx, and another branch to Clason's Point and Throg's Neck, as its original charter had specified. (The allure of this area is elusive, since it was thinly populated and consisted mostly of shoreline wetlands. Possibly the

The NYW&B included this "Proposed Station" drawing in its original promotional material. The train of IRT-style cars seems to be emerging from a long subway—and it also appears to be about to collide with a train in the station. Author's collection.

branch had been a charter requirement to provide developmental access, or perhaps the promoters saw their own real estate development opportunities.) In addition, it retained the 1872 provision for a branch from Pelham to White Plains and Elmsford, which, as located in 1905, would have closely followed the White Plains Post Road through Tuckahoe and Scarsdale, putting it almost next door to the New York Central's Harlem Division. (According to the promoters' map, however, the company only intended to build as far as White Plains, leaving little Elmsford to the New York Central's Putnam Division.) Aside from the White Plains line, though, the NYW&B's route virtually overlaid the New York & Port Chester's, beginning in the Bronx at 132nd Street and the Harlem River, connecting at East 177th Street with the planned subway, and passing through the shoreline towns of New Rochelle, Larchmont, Mamaroneck, and Rye. But intriguingly, the promoters' map showed its line extending just beyond Port Chester to the Connecticut border, poised to continue eastward.

Also like the New York & Port Chester, the New York, Westchester & Boston, according to its literature, was to "build a first-class four-track railroad of the very best construction known to engineering science, over private fenced-in right-of-way, with no grade crossings... equipped with the third-rail electric system for operating trains.... Track and rolling stock are to be electrically equipped similar to the New York Subway and the Manhattan Elevated Railroad." Its plan, said Bull, was to run direct service from Westchester County "through to the Battery" via its rapid transit connections in the Bronx.[7] The

Despite the previous drawing, the NYW&B actually planned this car for its services. Although dated January 1905, the drawing shows a car remarkably similar to (albeit somewhat longer than) L. B. Stillwell's original 1908 Hudson & Manhattan Railroad car fleet. Although the drawing is anonymously labeled "Office of Electrical Engineer," it seems likely that Stillwell was responsible. Later he designed the "new" New Haven–controlled NYW&B's fleet. Author's collection.

company itself seemed uncertain exactly what that equipment would look like, however. In its promotional material, one illustration depicted a train of steel cars almost identical to the Interborough Rapid Transit Company's new subway stock, designed for floor-level platforms, but with vestibule steps and end doors only. A more prophetic drawing, dated January 1905, showed a 55-foot-long car seating 64 passengers, with arched windows and center doors in addition to the two end doors, much like the equipment built soon thereafter for William G. McAdoo's new Hudson & Manhattan Railroad.

The situation immediately descended into chaos. The moment that Gotshall found out that the Westchester group seriously intended to build their road, he began legal proceedings on the basis that their charter was invalid because the company had been dormant for more than 30 years and in receivership most of that time.[8] The Westchester filed countersuits, and a free-for-all began that involved the New York City Board of Aldermen (with Tammany Democrats supporting the Westchester, and Republicans supporting the Port Chester) and the state legislature, with all the implications of bribery, payoffs, and legal obstruction that seemed traditional in the city's politics. The Westchester promoters were more successful fund-raisers and money disbursers, and with Tammany's help they received a franchise to cross the streets of the Bronx in 1904; a year later they had a similar franchise in Mount Vernon.[9] The New York & Port

A Deep Fog Descends ◉ 23

Chester already had acquired those rights in New Rochelle, but apparently was not able to show the New York City aldermen enough cash to change their minds, and it was not until 1906 that it was finally able to get its Bronx permits.[10]

Along the way, there were other dubious deals. In the words of historian and former New Haven official John Weller, "On April 25, 1904, one Charles H. Smith, a Chicago promoter, was awarded a contract to construct the New York, Westchester & Boston; only three days later he was given $1,050,000 cash and a like amount of Westchester stock to relinquish it. . . . A little later, another contractor named James P. McDonald was enriched by $375,000 for giving up his construction contract, on which he had done no work whatever." (Actually, McDonald did do about $169,000 worth of grading in the Bronx between 1905 and 1906.) Weller goes on to note that at one point the Westchester group tried a statesmanlike resolution by offering to buy 75 percent interest in the Gotshall group's Railroad & Development Company, giving it a 100 percent profit, only to discover afterward that the company had no binding contract with the New York & Port Chester and was worthless as a pawn.[11]

Despite all this, both companies issued stock and bonds, using most of the money to fight one another, but also in buying real estate and actually starting construction—the latter mostly to strengthen their legal positions. The Westchester company's New York City franchise required that it spend $1 million on construction (excluding right-of-way purchases) within two years of the franchise date, which was August 2, 1904. Work was slow to start, but on June 3, 1905, and without ceremony, the company

The original NYW&B promoters did some heavy grading and built several overpasses in the northeastern Bronx in 1906, including this long, skewed deck-girder bridge structure at Boston Road. Although somewhat lighter than later Westchester structures, it survived to the end. It is seen here two days before service ended in December 1937. George Votava photo, David Keller archive.

24 ◦ *The New York, Westchester & Boston Railway*

began its four-track grading in the thinly settled upper Bronx in the area between Pelham Parkway and Dyre Avenue, near the city line. As the August 2, 1906, deadline approached, the work became even more frenzied. Considerable grading was done in the area, and eight heavy highway overpasses were either fully or largely completed by then—specifically at Oakley Street, White Plains Road, Baychester Avenue, Boller Avenue, Brown Avenue, Saw Mill Lane, Givan Avenue, and a long, skewed seven-span deck girder structure over the Boston Post Road. Steelwork for 10 other bridges was on hand, but as of August 2, work had not yet begun. (By the photographic evidence, however, steelwork was fully erected for at least two of these—at East 222nd Street and Dyre Avenue—by October.) According to chief engineer Pratt, enough rail, ties, and other track materials were on hand to complete a full four-track line (including the electric third rail) within the Bronx. The $1 million requirement was met—barely. But this effort evidently drained the treasury, and progress promptly ended.[12]

For his part, Gotshall did what could only be called token grading in Harrison in 1906, and, among other things, completed a small concrete arch bridge over the creek dividing Harrison and Mamaroneck, a structure that survives today in isolated obscurity, still bearing the legend "N. Y. & P. R. R. 1906."[13]

By 1906, the legal situation had settled into a quagmire, with large amounts of money spent in the courts and "elsewhere," but with no tangible assets to show for it other than real estate and the construction noted. What induced supposedly rational bankers and investors to pour so much money into this sordid, unpromising affair is an enduring mystery, particularly considering that if either company chanced to succeed, it would have been largely redundant to existing lines anyway.

Two such bankers were Oakleigh Thorne and Marsden J. Perry, presidents of New York's Trust Company of America and the Union Trust Company of Rhode Island, respectively. Thorne, as his patrician-sounding name implied, came from New York banking blood and knew Morgan; his bank was one of New York's largest. Perry had risen from clog dancer and pawnbroker to a politically well connected Rhode Island financial power. A close associate of the powerful Senator Nelson W. Aldrich (who, in turn, was a key Morgan political ally), Perry was part of the state's corrupt political machine that controlled its politics and patronage and owned most of its public utilities. Among his interests were the Rhode Island trolley systems, which he and Aldrich controlled, and which Aldrich unloaded onto the New Haven in 1906 for about two and a half times their actual investment cost.[14]

Both Thorne and Perry had backed the New York, Westchester & Boston project as underwriters and had subsequently extended loans to support the court battles. Another New York bank, Charles T. Barney's Knickerbocker Trust Company, acted as trustee for the Westchester's bonds and had also loaned it $750,000 in mid-1906. Unfortunately, by 1906 both the Westchester and Port Chester projects were fast reaching the end of the road. The Westchester, for one, was heading toward receivership, with heavy debts and defaulted underwriting commitments, directly affecting Thorne's and Perry's banks as well as the Knickerbocker Trust.[15]

On January 26, 1906, the *Wall Street Journal* announced that Thorne, Perry, and other backers had taken over the Westchester project, with Perry acting as president. Looking to unload his albatross, Thorne approached the New Haven's Charles S. Mellen later in 1906, offering control of both the Westchester and the Port Chester ventures. With Mellen scooping up steamship and streetcar lines at almost any price, he seemed a likely mark. In this case, though, the New Haven president was properly unimpressed—or so he claimed later—seeing little competitive danger to his company from either project and no reason to bail out their backers.

To Mellen, that seemed to be that. Not so for Thorne, who pleaded with Mellen to take the proposition to the next New Haven directors' meeting. Fully expecting board disinterest, Mellen reluctantly agreed and introduced it at the September 12 meeting. To his astonishment, Morgan moved to appoint a three-man special committee to study the matter and authorize stock purchases it deemed necessary. Although this unique committee would be responsible to no one and could spend what it wanted without any review, the compliant board bowed to Morgan and offered no objections. Mellen then dutifully appointed Morgan and his two closest board associates, William Rockefeller and lawyer George MacCulloch Miller, with himself as an ex-officio member.[16]

The "special committee" studied the matter with blinding speed. An October 2 meeting with Thorne was followed by a contract with Thorne and Perry on December 4, authorizing them to spend whatever was necessary to acquire for the New Haven at least 66 percent of the stock in all the companies described as "the Harlem River–Port Chester competition." The two bankers themselves would receive a 7.5 percent commission of anything they spent, with no maximum limit and no questions asked. Details of the transactions were to be kept completely secret, not only from the outside world but also from the New Haven board itself. Mellen was instructed to supply the needed money from the New Haven's treasury, placing it into a "Special Account No. 2" at J. P. Morgan & Company for Thorne and Perry to draw from. Morgan's personal attorney, Francis Lynde Stetson, represented all three parties to the contract—an odd arrangement under normal circumstances, but in this case it kept everything within a tight, secretive circle of presumably trusting partners.

The two bankers were at work well before their contract was signed. Stetson had advised Thorne and Perry to incorporate themselves in order to facilitate the New Haven's eventual purchase of their securities. Thus appeared the Millbrook Company, incorporated in early November 1906. (Thorne needed no deep thought to come up with a name for the new company. Millbrook honored the small town in the hills of rural Dutchess County, New York, that was the seat of his ancestral country estate where he soon retired, at age 46, to become a gentleman farmer, lord of the local manor, fox hunter, and breeder of horses and prize livestock. All that seemed to have a more salutary effect than banking, and he died there in 1948 at age 81.)

Between October 1906 and January 1907, Thorne and Perry—and later Millbrook—proceeded to disburse some $8.2 million in New Haven funds, gathering up large amounts of both the Westchester's and Port Chester's almost worthless stock, as well as that of several associated real estate and construction companies. Another $2.9 million went to the cause between January and October 29, 1907.[17]

Just as people began wondering why two supposedly hard-headed bankers were so interested in these insolvent enterprises, the Panic of 1907 hit Wall Street, and in the ensuing confusion, newspapers carried the report that Thorne had sold out to the New Haven. And indeed he had, although there had been much frantic scuffling behind the scenes beforehand.

Like many other major banks, Thorne's Trust Company of America had run into severe liquidity problems, as had the Knickerbocker Trust; both were suffering runs. The Knickerbocker collapsed, and its president, Charles Barney, shot himself. (Marsden Perry's bank subsequently succumbed in the panic, too, although Perry was made of sterner stuff than Charles Barney; he died in 1935 at age 84.) The run on Thorne's bank went out of control, and police were called in to control the mob of frightened depositors. In his efforts to quell the panic, Morgan pronounced that the Trust Company of America was "the place to stop the trouble." The New Haven was elected to help out by taking the Millbrook Company and its dubious assets off Thorne's hands in exchange for the $11.2 million that the New Haven had advanced it. Morgan's "Special Account No. 2" was summarily closed, and as of October 30, 1907, the New Haven directly controlled the New York, Westchester & Boston, the New York & Port Chester, and the City & County Contract Company.[18]

Thus far, the New Haven's board of directors had known nothing about the railroad's involvement with Thorne, Perry, the Millbrook Company, or "Special Account No. 2," and certainly had no idea of the money that had been spent. Morgan's three-man "special committee" had made no reports since it was formed over a year before. Some directors doubtless had wondered, but they knew not to ask. Now it was time for Morgan to say something.

What was said was brief, uninformative, but shocking. At a short November 9 board meeting, attorney Stetson simply stated that $11,155,000 had been expended for the Westchester and Port Chester properties. That was it. He did not explain where the money had gone or why it was spent. Stunned but acquiescent as always, the board unanimously approved the Morgan lawyer's report. But after the meeting, Mellen, who always had doubts about the undertaking, asked Morgan why there could not have been a bit more detail. In his best "I do not suffer fools gladly" mode, Morgan answered: "Did not Mr. Stetson draw up that vote? Do you think you know more how it ought to be done than he does?"[19]

Smarting under the rebuff and probably sensing trouble to come, Mellen penned this note on the back of his copy of the report:

> The trouble with this is that there is nothing to show who got the money for the truck turned over. I don't like the looks of it, and I don't see why the matter should not be made plain. If I had the stock and sold it, I should expect that others would state they bought it of me, but that don't seem to have been the situation here. I never have known the first thing about who originally held the securities, what they were sold for, and no one thought I was entitled to know. Perhaps I am not. I would feel better if there were at least a disposition to let me know something more than appears on the record.—C. S. M. 11-9-07.[20]

Other directors attending the meeting were equally dismayed and afterwards came to Mellen to object. Their conversations all ran similar to this one with director William Skinner:

Skinner: "Holy Caeserea Phillipi, what in the world have you been doing with $11 million of money [sic]?"

Mellen: "I will appoint you, Skinner, a committee to go find out."

Skinner: "Not on your life."[21]

During a far-reaching investigation of the New Haven's affairs in 1914 (more of which later), the Interstate Commerce Commission asked Mellen why the board had so meekly approved the report. He replied that everyone trusted Morgan's wisdom, however obscure it may be to mortals, and nobody wanted to pick a fight with him.[22] It should be remembered, too, that Morgan had just saved the country from the 1907 Panic by boldly calling up financial aid from every solvent institution in sight, and some simply assumed, incorrectly, that the New Haven was paying its fair share.

ICC accountants had also found that some $1,032,000 of the money spent had unaccountably disappeared. Called to testify at the same investigation, Oakleigh Thorne proved to be not only an amnesiac but also an astonishing example of banker incompetence, as displayed in this bit of sample testimony:

Governor Folk (conducting the investigation): "Did you give any vouchers for this $11 million?"

Thorne: "Any vouchers for it?"

Folk: "Yes."

Thorne: "No."

Folk: "Showing detailed expenditures."

Thorne: "No."

Folk: "You did not?"

Thorne: "No."[23]

It also turned out that when the Equitable Trust Company of New York acquired his bank in early 1912, Thorne decided to retire and burned all his personal books and records—"not wishing to keep on hand reminders of those trying days," as he said. Coincidentally, this occurred just before the series of investigations had begun, but Thorne did recall that much of the Westchester stock he had purchased came via "people on 14th Street," meaning Tammany Hall. He also managed to remember the less-trying $1,060,000 that he and Perry had received as their commissions.[24]

And what did the New Haven get for its $11 million? No more than about $4.9 million was carried on the books as what could be called tangible assets—mostly real estate, but including $1.4 million for the bits of construction already mentioned. Also included were various franchises, particularly within the Bronx. How much real value all of that represented was anyone's guess. The rest mostly went into the mists, although the ICC was able to trace $1.6 million to the Gotshall group for New York & Port Chester stock, $4.1 million to Westchester bondholders, $816,250 to the Knickerbocker Trust Company for construction company notes, and $2.4 million to City & County Contract Company stockholders.[25] (Gotshall, incidentally, was no shadowy promoter. He became a world renowned railroad builder and rebuilder who lectured on the subject. He was interested in biology, geology, and archaeology, did archaeological research in Palestine, spoke five languages, and was a champion fencer as well as a wide reader and bibliophile who donated his books to the New York State Library.)

Be that as it may, everyone now naturally assumed that with the New Haven in control, these two plainly unnecessary lines would be put to death speedily. But logic got a swift comeuppance in the New Haven's annual stockholder report for its fiscal year ending June 30, 1908. In it, Mellen began by owning up to what had already happened:

> An investment amounting to $10,955,000 was made during the year ending June 30, 1908, in the Millbrook Company.

Good so far, although stockholders who kept up with the business news might have paused at that point to wonder why such a sum had been spent on two promotional ventures that had few assets and nebulous charter and franchise rights. But then:

This control was obtained with the intention of completing the construction of either the New York and Port Chester Railroad, or the New York, Westchester and Boston Railroad, substantially in accordance with the original plans, and the work of construction will be prosecuted vigorously as soon as the litigation in which the New York, Westchester and Boston is involved can be terminated.

So the New Haven actually intended to carry out one of those schemes and build a four-track electric railroad that almost exactly duplicated its own. Furthermore, more money already was being spent:

This investment has been increased during the year ended June 30, 1908, by the amount of $807,483.20 for additional securities of the Millbrook Company acquired, which company is the direct owner of all the other companies mentioned. The total amount of our investment in this account on June 30, 1908, was $11,762,483.20.[26]

Mellen neglected to explain just why the New Haven was doing this and what it might ultimately cost. He implied, though, that even before building this baffling new railroad, still more money would be needed to clear up lawsuits and other vague matters.

Curiouser and curiouser, as Alice remarked.

Heavy NYW&B girders are being very carefully lowered over the New Haven's 11,000-volt AC catenary at Columbus Avenue, Mount Vernon, in 1911. Harry F. Brown photo, Jack W. Swanberg collection.

3

BUILDING THE PERFECT RAILROAD, 1909–1912

As Mellen mentioned in his 1908 annual report, building this new railroad was still some time and money away. Buying the controlling stock of the two projects—by whatever the means—was one thing; clearing up the clouded franchises and other messy legal matters was something else. Unraveling all that seemed extremely difficult until it was mentioned that some 34,000 shares of the New York, Westchester & Boston company were still outstanding—reputedly handed out to politicians and other "people of influence" during its battles with the Port Chester. Then, sometime in 1908, a former New York police inspector named Thomas J. Byrnes called on Mellen. Byrnes intimated that the missing stock could be delivered and the legal difficulties cleared up if some sort of "agreement" could be reached.[1] It turned out that an additional $1.5 million, over and above what the New Haven had paid for the Thorne-Perry purchases, would do the trick. (Mellen later stated that he assumed Byrnes represented Tammany Hall, although in fact Byrnes was a Republican. Nonetheless, Mellen was probably correct.)

Concealing that payout called for more financial sleight of hand, an art that Mellen had already perfected. On June 15, 1908, the New Haven transferred 8,000 shares of its treasury stock, worth $150 a share, to its subsidiary, the New England Navigation Company. The steamship company then generously gave the stock to Mellen personally. On March 5, 1909, another 1,495 New Haven shares followed the same devious route. Mellen also received some substantial cash advances.

In the meantime, the New Haven's attorney, Charles F. Choate Jr., had put together a list of "thirteen things" that had to be resolved to clear everything up. Mellen began making payments of New Haven stock or cash (often in small bills) to mysterious messengers who periodically appeared at his New York office to turn over the old NYW&B stock and receive his personal promissory notes. Other unknowns would then collar him in places like hotel lobbies, present the notes, and be paid in cash. After receiving the Westchester securities—"not worth ten cents a pound," in Mellen's words—he would deposit them in the New Haven's treasury to replace the stock that had been removed. Adding this latest bundle to what Thorne and Perry had already bought, the New Haven now found itself the owner of over 99 percent of the New York,

Westchester & Boston's stock issue. The "thirteen things"—consisting of legal changes and franchise clarifications—were quickly and mysteriously taken care of, and the New Haven could now build its redundant super-railroad.

As with the Thorne-Perry-Millbrook dealings, nobody seemed to know where the money went. Asked during the ICC's 1914 investigation, Mellen professed to have known none of the people he paid; the only name he produced was former inspector Byrnes, who, unfortunately, was unable to testify on account of his earlier death.[2]

In all, the New Haven had now disbursed some $14 million in order to be allowed to spend considerably more to compete with itself. But at least everything was now in order, and on December 31, 1909, the New York, Westchester & Boston and the New York & Port Chester were corporately merged. The New York State Public Service Commission approved the consolidation less than a month later, on January 19, 1910.

Since the old NYW&B had a broader charter, now-clear franchises, and some substantial construction, the New Haven used its corporate shell as the surviving company, also retaining its name. The "new" New York, Westchester & Boston Railway, now in its second rebirth, was capitalized at $5 million in stock (99.6 percent of it owned by the New Haven) and $60 million in bonds—the interest and principal of which were to be guaranteed by the New Haven. Since the New Haven already owned virtually all of the stock, and no more was ever issued, any construction would be financed entirely through bonds. The initial bond issue amounted to $21.2 million, of which the New Haven itself took about 10 percent, upping its direct Westchester investment by another $2.2 million. (By 1930 this had increased to $3.15 million.) As it turned out, the new company's funded debt would never exceed $22.4 million, although plenty of other debts would be forthcoming, mostly in the form of advances from the New Haven.

To head the Westchester company, the New Haven picked Leverett Saltonstall Miller, the general manager of its newly acquired Central New England subsidiary. At age 46, Miller had been around. A graduate of Rensselaer Polytechnic Institute, he had held various engineering and management jobs on the Denver, Utah & Pacific and the Colorado Railroad (both of them CB&Q affiliates), the Eastern Alabama, Erie, Tennessee Central, St. Paul & Duluth, Central Washington, and Seattle & International—the last three absorbed by the Northern Pacific. He finally came to rest on the New Haven in 1904 when it took over the Central New England, and from there he went to the Westchester presidency in 1909. More to the point, though, Miller was the son of George MacCulloch Miller, a New York corporate lawyer, close Morgan friend, New Haven director, and a member of Morgan's secretive "special committee," which had directed the Westchester and New York & Port Chester purchase. Leverett Miller was said to be a charming man, perhaps not surprising given his breeding. While his railroad career may have been footloose, his blood was decidedly blue. Besides his own family's wealth (the MacCulloch Millers lived a well-upholstered life as the toast of Morristown, New Jersey, society), he was a close relative of the Massachusetts Saltonstalls, a Boston Brahmin clan that stretched back to the *Mayflower* and produced Leverett A. Saltonstall, the flinty-faced Massachusetts governor (1939–1945) and U.S. senator (1945–1967).[3]

That charm, along with his optimism and salesmanship, would be needed soon enough, but for the moment Miller was given the enviable job of building a state-of-the-art super-railroad from scratch, without regard to cost and without asking questions.

Miller had free rein to borrow the New Haven's electrical and civil engineers for design work and construction supervision, and he hired the St. Paul, Minnesota, architectural firm of Reed & Stem to design the structures and to serve as general consultants. Despite its seeming midwestern obscurity, Reed & Stem already was well connected with the New York Central (Charles Reed's sister was married to William Wilgus, the Central's chief engineer) and had been the original architects of the new Grand Central Terminal. (By 1909 the firm had been forced to share Grand Central's design work with Whitney Warren's firm, Warren & Wetmore. By yet another coincidence, Warren, although highly talented in his own right, was a cousin of William K. Vanderbilt.)[4]

Alfred Fellheimer, then a Reed & Stem junior partner and one of Grand Central's planners, was put in charge of the Westchester project. After conferring with Miller, the 35-year-old Fellheimer learned some amazing things. He found that the New York, Westchester & Boston was to be a fully developed, high-speed, high-capacity railroad, the major part of which was to run through practically virgin territory. Everything on it was to be of the highest quality available, down to tie bolts and spikes; no concessions to economy were in order. Solid, commodious, and attractive stations were to be built almost literally in the middle of nowhere. Already well versed in the theory and practice of railway location and construction, Fellheimer protested that railroads simply do not spring up fully grown in this manner, and he suggested that the Westchester be built more economically and upgraded as its territory developed and its traffic increased. No, said Miller. He had been instructed to build the best suburban railway possible. He admitted, though, that he had questioned the idea himself and found that even when his New Haven superiors brought up the Westchester project, they were met with rolled eyes and told to "go see J. P. Morgan."[5]

It will be remembered that the original New York, Westchester & Boston's charter envisioned a main line between the Harlem River and Port Chester, with branches to Throg's Neck in the Bronx and to Elmsford via White Plains. In the New Haven's somewhat edited version, the Port Chester mainline would temporarily end at New Rochelle, to be completed to Port Chester at some vague later date and over a yet-undetermined route, using either the New Haven's mainline right-of-way or one of the alignments planned by its predecessor companies. Under a New York State law preceding the merger, the New York Public Service Commission required all branches to be built, but the New Haven was able to get permission to shed the Clason's Point–Throg's Neck Branch as well as the White Plains–Elmsford section of the White Plains Branch, neither of which would have served much of anything. The law and the PSC insisted on a Mount Vernon–White Plains line, though, and the New Haven apparently did not try to contest it. That decision was a bit surprising, since White Plains was not in New Haven territory, and the projected route passed through no intermediate points of any note. But by then the New Haven already was thinking of another use for the line.

Alignment changes were made in the 1904 NYW&B company's planned route. Since some substantial construction had already been done there, the original route through the northern part of the Bronx was kept as originally intended, but from 174th Street south to the Harlem River the line was to use the New Haven's Harlem River Branch right-of-way rather than a projected separate alignment to its west. And north of the New York City–Westchester County line, the original route was almost completely revised to pass through less-developed territory where property acquisition and construction would be cheaper.

So, as its "first phase" route was finally established, the Westchester was to be 21.7 miles long. Eighteen miles were on its own property, and the rest were on the New Haven's. Its southern terminal was to be the New Haven's Harlem River station at 132nd Street in the Bronx, alongside the river and near the Interborough Rapid Transit Company's Third Avenue elevated line. (Although the New Haven had abandoned its through service into Manhattan over the el spur in 1905, the IRT still operated a shuttle between the railroad terminal and the 129th Street station of the Second and Third Avenue el lines in Manhattan.) From there, it would use two tracks on the New Haven Harlem River Branch right-of-way as far as East 174th Street, serving NH stations at Port Morris, Casanova, Hunt's Point, and Westchester Avenue. Already, the New Haven was rebuilding the entire branch between New Rochelle and the river for six tracks, partly for Westchester use but more importantly in anticipation of the planned Hell Gate Bridge connection with Penn Station in Manhattan and new harbor freight transfer facilities in the Bay Ridge section of Brooklyn. (The monumental Hell Gate project itself was begun in 1911 and completed in 1917.)

At East 174th Street, the Westchester diverged onto its own four-track right-of-way, passing a combination express station and general office building at East 180th Street and Morris Park Avenue, and proceeding northward along the original NYW&B company's partially built route through a thinly populated section of the eastern Bronx. After crossing the Westchester County line, the four tracks continued through the east side of Mount Vernon, with a local station at East Sixth Street and Fulton Avenue, a major express station at East Third and Fulton, and another local stop where the line crossed the New Haven's Grand Central mainline at its Columbus Avenue station.

Just north of the Westchester's Columbus Avenue station, the four tracks divided in a "Y" pattern into two double-track branches, one turning east to New Rochelle and the other heading north to White Plains. (The original NYW&B had placed its junction on the south side of Mount Vernon, with its New Rochelle Branch touching the older section of Pelham south of the New Haven mainline.)

As revised, the New Rochelle Branch, actually considered the main line, followed a back-door route through the far north side of Pelham and the outer portions of downtown New Rochelle, crossing Webster Avenue at Sickles and ending at North Avenue somewhat north of the city's center. Although regular train operations ended at the North Avenue station, the two tracks continued eastward to a track connection with the New Haven's mainline at what was known as Larchmont Junction. Between New Rochelle and Port Chester, the planned (but postponed) mainline eventually was built alongside the New Haven's tracks through Larchmont, Mamaroneck, and Rye. Most of this section already had been graded for extra tracks.

The White Plains Branch struck out through mostly woods and farms. This route occupied a sparsely settled no-man's land located in the area between the built-up communities along the New York Central's Harlem Division and those on the New Haven's mainline along Long Island Sound shore. Indeed, unlike the 1904 plan, it appeared that the Westchester's engineers deliberately tried to avoid encroaching on the Central's immediate market area by locating the line between a mile and a half and two miles to its east. The route followed the Hutchinson River through Wykagyl, on North Avenue at the far west border of New Rochelle, then cross-country through what later became Quaker Ridge and Heathcote, on the far east side of Scarsdale. (Heathcote's name honored Colonel Caleb Heathcote, the early eighteenth-century proprietor of the Manor of Scarsdale, which made up all of present Scarsdale as well as most of Mamaroneck.

Scarsdale, in turn, was named for Heathcote's home district in England.)[6] The branch ended on what was then the eastern edge of White Plains's commercial center at Westchester Avenue and Bloomingdale Road.

With all the corporate and organizational pieces now expensively in place, construction was pushed with some urgency. Contractors' bids were opened in July 1909, even before the companies had been formally merged, and additional real estate acquisition proceeded quickly. As was too often the case with such projects, some shady politicians obtained right-of-way maps, bought up some of the land in its path, and threw up jerry-built "apartment houses" to sell to the railroad at exorbitant prices. And, as Fellheimer put it, he and the other engineers and contractors "spent money like drunken sailors."[7]

Whatever the haste and cost, a magnificent specimen of railroad emerged, extolled by virtually every professional trade magazine in the engineering and transportation fields. Following the original concept, there were no grade crossings. The tracks were carried over and under roads with 43 steel railroad bridges, 23 highway bridges, four concrete arches, and a four-track cut-and-cover subway north of Morris Park station in the Bronx measuring close to 4,000 feet long. (The subway was a franchise requirement to pass under Pelham Parkway and allow a roadway along the top of the line that became the Esplanade.) Exceptionally heavy steel viaducts crossed the New Haven mainline and a street at Mount Vernon, the Hutchinson River just north of there, and Bronx streets south of the 180th Street station. (As part of its construction, the new line incorporated the grading and Bronx highway overpasses that the original Westchester company had built in 1906. These bridges were of somewhat lighter construction than those the Westchester adopted, but were adequate for its immediate use—and, in fact, were never replaced or rebuilt.)

Projected through hilly and rocky terrain, the Westchester's right-of-way was almost never on level ground. To keep curvature and grades to a minimum, construction crews blasted out numerous deep rock cuts and piled up high earth fills. Over three-quarters of the line's mileage required such work—7 of the railroad's 21 miles were in cuts averaging 16 feet deep, while 9 miles were on fills or embankments with an average height of 14 feet. Thanks to all this, the line's sharpest curve was six degrees and, with two short exceptions, the steepest grade was one percent. The track structure consisted of 90-pound rail atop deep stone ballast and was designed for speeds up to 60 mph.[8]

The electrification method was a critical issue. Both the 1904 NYW&B company and New York & Port Chester intended to use a 600-volt DC third-rail system that was compatible with the city rapid transit lines and that in slightly modified form was also used by the New York Central. Despite its drawbacks, this was economically appropriate for the Westchester's short-distance system and would have allowed possible future use of the subway lines to reach into Manhattan. The New Haven, on the other hand, had completed the first phase of its 11,000-volt, 25 hz. AC mainline electrification in 1907, including its own new high-capacity generating plant at Cos Cob, Connecticut. By 1910 its engineers were experienced in the system's installation and operation, and at the time, the Cos Cob plant had extra capacity. Whether there was any serious debate about which system to use is now unknown, but if so, compatibility with the New Haven won out. Even so, some refinements were made. Rather than the unique and expensive to maintain triangular catenary design that the New Haven had installed between Woodlawn and Stamford, both the Westchester and the New Haven's Harlem River Branch were electrified using a compound catenary system that

Unquestionably, the Westchester's most impressive structure was this heavy trestle-girder bridge combination at Columbus Avenue in Mount Vernon. The view looks southwest from the New Haven's Grand Central mainline, seen at the right. A northbound local is slowing for the Columbus Avenue local station while an express overtakes it on the four-track line. George Votava photo, Dave Keller archive.

A short distance north and east of the Columbus Avenue trestle, this curved span carried the double-track New Rochelle Branch over the Hutchinson River valley. The photographer is aiming northwest as a two-car Port Chester express glides across in October 1937. In the distance at the right is a catenary tower for the White Plains Branch. Alfred Seibel photo, author's collection.

The hilly White Plains Branch required some deep rock cuts, such as this one at Wykagyl, shown in December 1937. George Votava photo, Bob's Photo collection.

High fills were needed, too, such as this one on the New Rochelle line in Pelham. The 1912 photo looks west toward the Hutchinson River viaduct. Harry F. Brown photo, author's collection.

Building the Perfect Railroad ◉ 37

Even road overpasses got the built-for-eternity treatment. This concrete arch span took Bryant Avenue over the line in White Plains. It still does, although the cut below has been partially filled in and nature has otherwise taken over. Harry F. Brown photo, author's collection.

became the industry standard. As an experiment, however, single catenary was installed on part of the New Rochelle Branch east of the Columbus Avenue junction in Mount Vernon. (Apparently it was not deemed appropriate for running-track use, since later extensions used the compound system.) As was standard practice at the time, copper messenger wires fed a steel contact wire, but pantograph action created rust particles that soon discolored the car roofs and sides, and copper was substituted in 1923. Under the original installation, power was transmitted from the Cos Cob plant (which at the time had plenty of extra capacity) and delivered to the Westchester at Larchmont Junction, where the Westchester right-of-way met the New Haven mainline east of the New Rochelle station. A single substation, located at the Columbus Avenue junction, distributed the power from there. (The Cos Cob–New Rochelle feed was replaced in 1915 with commercial power purchased from New York Edison and delivered at the West Farms–174th Street junction with the Harlem River Branch.)[9]

Signaling also basically followed the system used in the New Haven's new electrified zone, mostly using distinctive stub-bladed two-position semaphores suspended from the catenary support towers and arranged so that they would be as near as practical to the motorman's eye level. Automatic block signal spacing anticipated five-

The NYW&B's four-track mainline through the upper Bronx was straight and fast. Now reduced to two outer tracks and minus the 11,000-volt AC overhead catenary, this section still survives as a branch of the Lexington Avenue subway. Harry F. Brown photo, author's collection.

minute rush hour service headways or less, and both track and signaling were designed for speeds up to 57 mph. Italian Renaissance–style towers with high arched windows controlled six interlocking plants: Baychester Avenue in the Bronx, the Columbus Avenue junction in Mount Vernon, the White Plains and New Rochelle terminals, and on the White Plains Branch at Wykagyl and Heathcote stations. A seventh interlocking was housed in the 180th Street station building. (New Haven towers controlled train movements at the Harlem River terminal, Oak Point, and the West Farms–174th Street junction.) The Wykagyl and Heathcote interlockings each controlled a pair of passing tracks located at the stations themselves, plus a freight spur at each point. The original idea of these 1,500-foot-long passing sidings, together with another pair just west of the North Avenue station at New Rochelle, was to allow rush hour expresses to overtake and pass locals stopped at the stations. But this bit of optimism quickly faded, and the Wykagyl and Heathcote passing tracks were stub-ended and downgraded to freight switching leads and holding tracks. Both New Rochelle sidings were also later stub-ended and used for off-hour car storage. The Baychester Avenue plant controlled a set of three crossovers on the four-track section, originally thought useful to facilitate close rush hour express and local train operation as well as emergencies—but this, too, proved unneeded and was closed and the crossovers removed. An elaborate Western Electric closed telephone communications network connected dispatchers, interlocking towers, and all stations—one of the first such private phone systems anywhere.[10]

Building the Perfect Railroad ⦿ 39

This heavy single-arm catenary support was used for the extended freight spur at the White Plains terminal. The 1922 photo looks north toward the freight yard, about three blocks away. Harry F. Brown photo, author's collection.

While the Westchester's electrification, signaling, and track structure followed the New Haven's latest practice, its cars, structures, and fare collection system were emphatically and distinctively its own.

By the time construction started in 1909, electric multiple-unit equipment had become standard on urban elevated and subway systems as well as several suburban railroad services—not only the New York Central and New Haven, but such diverse operations as the Long Island Rail Road, the Northwestern Pacific, the Pennsylvania Railroad's West Jersey & Seashore subsidiary, and the Southern Pacific's Oakland electrification, then under way. Rapid transit and railroad suburban car design differed, though. New York Central and New Haven "m.u." cars, for example, were essentially electric versions of conventional railroad coaches, heavier and up to 20 feet longer than comparable subway and el equipment. And while rapid transit cars had

The Westchester's junction with the New Haven's Harlem River Branch at East 174th Street in the West Farms section of the Bronx, as it looked shortly after the line opened in 1912. The view looks north; the NYW&B line diverges at the left beyond newly built New Haven tower SS8. In later years the junction track layout was substantially simplified. Harry F. Brown photo, author's collection.

sliding doors and floor-level platform loading, railroad m.u.'s were designed for traditional ground-level platforms and loaded through steps and hinged end vestibule doors. (The only major exception at this time was the Illinois Central's steam-powered Chicago suburban system, which used high-level platforms.)

In keeping with its "newest and best" philosophy, the Westchester decided to depart from the railroad standard and combine the best elements of rapid transit and railroad practice in a car that would have the carrying capacity and comfort of full-length railroad coaches coupled with subway loading and unloading efficiency. But the combination of standard railroad dimensions for its cars and the 11,000-volt AC electrification system precluded any thought of future through operation over the city subways.

To design his new fleet, Miller went to Lewis B. Stillwell, a consulting electrical engineer who had done work for the Manhattan Railway, the Interborough Rapid Transit subway, William Gibbs McAdoo's new Hudson & Manhattan Railroad (the "Hudson Tubes"—now PATH), and several electric lines elsewhere. Stillwell had recently designed a new type of steel car framing for the Hudson & Manhattan's equipment that promised greater strength and comparatively lighter weight. (There is evidence that Stillwell may have drawn the preliminary plans for the original Westchester company's cars in 1905, which were to have been very similar to the Hudson & Manhattan's.) Using his basic H&M car structure, Stillwell produced a 70-foot, 60-ton all-steel m.u. car for the Westchester, seating 78 passengers, with three sets of pneumatically operated sliding doors on each side—two conventional end doors and a subway-style center door—for use with the company's standard high-level station platforms. (The end platforms also had conventional traps and steps, needed at stations on the New Haven's Harlem River Branch, as well as emergency use.) Two 175-hp Westinghouse single-phase AC motors carried in one truck could accelerate the cars at 1 mile per hour per second, and easily maintained the railroad's designed top speed of 57 mph—performance considered ideal for the planned service. The combination of the cars' weight and high service speeds required a specially designed, more powerful braking system combining both pneumatic and electric controls. (Ironically, the New Haven's contemporaneous m.u. cars—which, incidentally, were the only steel cars in its vast passenger fleet—not only were thoroughly conventional in design but had nineteenth-century open platforms.)

Externally, the new Westchester cars looked like nobody else's. Like Stillwell's shorter Hudson & Manhattan cars, their roofs had a unique curved monitor design incorporating faired headlights, giving them a clean, sleek appearance compared with conventional railroad coaches or m.u. cars. Windows were paired, with arches over each pair, making these thoroughly modern cars look oddly antique but unquestionably distinctive. Unlike typical railroad suburban cars, electric or not, the cars were fitted with end diaphragms to protect passengers while moving from car to car. (The Erie Railroad was so impressed by Stillwell's Westchester design that it later ordered large quantities of similar coaches for its steam-powered suburban network.)[11]

For its initial services, the Westchester ordered 30 such cars from Pittsburgh's Pressed Steel Car Company—28 coaches and 2 coach-baggage combines seating 54. (Enough baggage and express business to warrant specialized cars never materialized, and in 1922 the two cars were rebuilt as full coaches.) Over the next 16 years, some 65

Car 113, typical of the Westchester's entire fleet, pauses at Baychester Avenue station in the Bronx in 1937. George Votava photo, Bob's Photo collection.

additional cars were built to the same basic specifications and outward appearance, differing primarily in minor dimensional details and seating two more passengers. In a further flush of optimism, five of these were originally ordered as trailers for use in trains of five cars or more, but finding that they were poorly utilized, the Westchester motorized them in 1928.

Rounding out the Westchester's roster was an all-purpose self-powered gas-electric line and crane car (a very early application of this type of power), four work cars, and a single Baldwin-Westinghouse 520-hp center-cab electric locomotive. Almost identical to the New Haven's 0200-class (later EY-2) switchers, this little "motor" did all the railroad's grunt work, handling its light freight business, work trains, shop switching, and whatever else came along. It could run in multiple with its New Haven siblings and occasionally did so. Any other service equipment needs were met by renting cars, cabooses, and—very rarely—wrecking cranes from the New Haven.

Each Westchester station was individually designed to provide an aesthetically fitting focal point for the upper-class communities it was expected to develop. All were faced with concrete to present a spotless appearance and cut maintenance costs, with steel framing and masonry shells (primarily ceramic block) beneath; many were made integral with the cuts, fills, and bridges at their sites. All had commodious interiors finished in terrazzo, and at least eight had elevators and station space for handling express and checked baggage. (Those known were at the Harlem River terminal, 180th Street, East Third Street in Mount Vernon, Chester Heights, Wykagyl, Heathcote, and the Westchester Avenue terminal in White Plains.) As part of their hoped-for role as community centers—and to generate revenue at the same time—many stations also provided for commercial space.

At the time, adaptations of "period" architectural styles such as Spanish, Italian, English Tudor, French chateau, and neoclassical were just coming into vogue in upper-class suburbs, and Fellheimer and Miller decided that harmonious variations of Mediterranean styles would make the railroad both distinctive and fashionable. The New Haven itself also was building some stations in these general styles. (As it developed, though, during the 1920s southern Westchester County most passionately embraced half-timbered Tudor buildings and a general English-inspired environment, making the Westchester's buildings even more distinctive and perhaps more exotic than originally planned.)

For the Westchester, Fellheimer used two basic Mediterranean design types—what he labeled as "modified Mission" and "simplified Italian Renaissance"—that featured various mixtures of curved upper windows, inset columns and arches, tile roofs, and white stucco-appearing outer surfaces (which, as noted, were actually concrete). Almost all were different from one another, although those at Pelham Parkway, East Sixth Street in Mount Vernon, Pelhamwood, and Webster Avenue in New Rochelle were closely similar "modified Mission" types. Basically, stations in the Bronx and between Mount Vernon and New Rochelle were variations on the more spare "modified Mission" style, while those on the White Plains Branch were "simplified Italian Renaissance" designs. But there were several exceptions. The imposing three-story station–general office building in the Bronx at East 180th Street (officially 481 Morris Avenue) was modeled on an Italian villa, with twin towers, an arcaded loggia, and red tile roofs; behind it, the steel viaduct carrying the tracks was faced over to be integral with the design. Pelham's Fifth Avenue station was a spectacular-looking affair, consisting of platforms on a huge fill integrated into a concrete archway over the street below. The important express-transfer station at East Third Street, Mount Vernon, got its own style, a blend of Italian and classical, with a skylighted arcade flanked by marble columns. And finally, there was Quaker Ridge, located on the White Plains Branch between Wykagyl and Heathcote, in a sparsely settled area the Westchester hoped to develop. Quaker Ridge station was in a class by itself and the most distinctive of any of its structures. Situated between the two mainline tracks, Quaker Ridge was a mixed neoclassical design that harked back to the 1893 Columbian Exposition, with Baroque buttress touches at its ground-level entranceway, a high vaulted ceiling, and large expanses of glass with arched upper windows topped by sculptured spandrels.

Concrete high-level platforms were standard at all stations, with Doric columns supporting the overhead canopies. (Several stations that had been built around earth fills were given "temporary" wood platforms until the fills settled. They settled, but the platforms were never rebuilt.) Platforms and cars were designed to work together to move high passenger volumes quickly; passengers walked directly onto the car floors through the three doors on each car side in an unimpeded flow. Floor-level platforms had been standard on urban rapid transit lines for years before, but with only a few exceptions—notably large terminals such as Grand Central and Penn Station, and the Illinois Central's Chicago suburban lines—they were almost unknown on steam railroads. Only since the late 1960s have they come into more common use for suburban operations and such high-capacity passenger services as Amtrak's Northeast Corridor.

Westchester station exteriors were adorned with cast concrete decorative motifs symbolizing speed, primarily variations and combinations of Mercury's caduceus and winged motifs. Heathcote station was unique in having a pair of crests flanking the doorway reproducing the coat-of-arms of Caleb Heathcote, Lord of the Manor of Scarsdale. As far as is known, no other station had decoration specifically related to the community. Architect Fellheimer's efforts were well received by the railroad world, for the trade magazine *Electric Railway Journal* applauded his stations, towers, and shop building as "constitut[ing] the most attractive group of way structures possessed by any electric or steam railroad in the United States."[12]

The four New Haven–owned local stations on the Harlem River Branch that the Westchester served were architecturally different, but fully as solid and some even more ornate—all newly built as part of the six-tracking and grade crossing elimination project carried out between 1904 and 1909, and designed by Cass Gilbert, renowned architect of New York's Woolworth Building. Unlike the Westchester's own stations, all these had traditional railroad-style track-level platforms, and as noted above, the Westchester cars had steps for use in this section. As befitting its surroundings, the Harlem River terminal station was by far the least aesthetic of the lot—an unpretentious facility incorporated in a large, long, undistinguished four-story brick New Haven office building.[13]

Westchester station interiors were laid out to accommodate the line's subway-style in-station fare collection system, which was unique to any American suburban railroad. The station agent sat in a booth beyond the waiting room; recessed turnstiles and gates on either side provided the only platform access. Boarding passengers passed through the turnstiles where their tickets were punched and returned to them. When exiting their destination station, they either dropped the ticket into a chopper box under the watch of a guard or, if they had a multi-ride ticket, presented it for inspection. The line

Looking east at the line's first terminal at North Avenue, New Rochelle, in 1912. The two long sidings in the foreground were intended for overnight car storage and to allow rush hour expresses to pass locals. They were soon stub-ended and used for storage. Harry F. Brown photo, author's collection.

was divided into fare zones, each of which had its own distinctively colored ticket so that any zone overriding was quickly spotted at the exits when an off-color ticket was offered. (There was an elaborate way to beat this system, but how many riders actually bothered is unknown.) Conductors and trainmen were thus freed from on-board ticket collection, theoretically making more efficient use of manpower, ensuring that all fares were collected, and allowing faster operations.[14]

The stations included another innovative touch: to warn waiting passengers that their train was about to arrive, waiting rooms had flashing lights activated when the train entered the station circuit.

All inspection, maintenance, and heavy repair work was done in a compact, cleanly designed shop located adjacent to Unionport Road, just north of the 180th Street station and office. Fellheimer may have done his best to visualize how Spanish missionaries would design a modern railroad shop, but instead he used a more practical stripped-down neoclassical style, with a family resemblance to his Quaker Ridge station. Aside from large arched windows on its front and rear façades and a high vaulted ceiling, the building was largely an exemplary example of utilitarian twentieth-century steel-and-concrete industrial architecture. Along with the front and rear windows, high and wide side windows provided generous natural lighting and ventilation. As originally built, the shop consisted of a three-track main shop, machine shop, and storehouse enclosed in a single building. A paint shop was added a year later, employing the brand-new technique of spray painting, rather than the hand brush method traditional in railroad shops. Shop layout and management was a model of efficiency. Although relatively small, the facility was designed to service an ultimate fleet of 100 cars by moving them in and out in half a day (wreck repairs and painting excepted). This was accomplished by keeping a full inventory close at hand for the rapid changeout of components and trucks. The system apparently worked. Although the Westchester's fleet eventually totaled 95 cars, its maintenance was always considered exceptional.[15] The shop complex also included a small storage yard.

In all, the Westchester's physical plant was designed and built for eternity, or at least the railroad equivalent thereof, and also would accommodate the heaviest loads into the far future. Would that it were to be.

AN NYW&B ARCHITECTURE GALLERY

This Italian villa housed the Westchester's general offices as well as the important East 180th Street subway transfer station. Located at 481 Morris Avenue at 180th Street, it survives today under New York MTA ownership and is on the National Register. George Votava photo, Dave Keller archive.

Next in importance was the express station at East Third Street in Mount Vernon, which served downtown Mount Vernon and passengers transferring between White Plains and New Rochelle–Port Chester trains. Reed & Fellheimer photo, 1912, from the collection of the late John Tolley, courtesy of Robert A. Bang.

The less aesthetic back side of the East Third Street station, looking north in 1921. Harry F. Brown photo, author's collection.

Westchester station interiors tended to be austere but spacious. Again at East Third Street, the photo looks from the waiting room to the agent's office and controlled access to the platforms. Passengers passed the agent and a turnstile at the right and exited to the left by the ticket inspector. Reed & Fellheimer photo, 1912, from the collection of the late John Tolley, courtesy of Robert A. Bang.

Wykagyl, on the White Plains Branch at the west corner of New Rochelle, was typical of Fellheimer's so-called Simplified Italian Renaissance style, used for all stations on this line. A single-track Westchester Electric R. R. trolley line passed on a dirt-paved North Avenue in front, and development awaited. Reed & Fellheimer photo, 1912, from the collection of the late John Tolley, courtesy of Robert A. Bang.

Another version of the Italian Renaissance style was at Mamaroneck Avenue in White Plains. Passengers could board Westchester Street R. R. trolleys here for downtown White Plains or Mamaroneck. Reed & Fellheimer photo, 1912, from the collection of the late John Tolley, courtesy of Robert A. Bang.

A small but undeniably spectacular station served Fifth Avenue in Pelham on the New Rochelle line. Another Westchester Electric trolley route passed the door. Reed & Fellheimer photo, 1912, from the collection of the late John Tolley, courtesy of Robert A. Bang.

The rear of Heathcote station on the White Plains Branch, looking north. Elevators for baggage and package freight were incorporated in the stairway structures, and at left a spur swung west to reach a small freight house. This area has since been demolished for a roadway, but the headhouse in the rear still stood (although endangered) in 2007. Reed & Fellheimer photo, 1912, from the collection of the late John Tolley, courtesy of Robert A. Bang.

The "Modified Mission" design of East Sixth Street station in Mount Vernon was repeated with slight variations at several other locations. Author's photo, 1952.

Interlocking towers also got the Renaissance treatment. HC tower stood northwest of the Heathcote passenger station and originally controlled two long passing sidings and a crossover. George Votava photo, 1937, Dave Keller archive.

An NYW&B Architecture Gallery

Quaker Ridge, south of Heathcote on the White Plains Branch, was unique in several ways and incorporated elements found in several large-city terminals of the time—such as Grand Central, which the architect also worked on. The quasi-neoclassical structure sat between the two tracks on a fill, with passengers entering through the buttressed passageway below. With its airy windows, the station later became an artist's residence. Reed & Fellheimer photo, 1912, from the collection of the late John Tolley, courtesy of Robert A. Bang.

Although not an NYW&B structure, the New Haven station at Hunt's Point, designed by Cass Gilbert, served Westchester local and express trains and, beginning in 1919, subway transfer passengers. New Haven passenger service ended in 1930, but the station continued in NYW&B use through 1937. NYNH&H RR photo, c. 1910, author's collection.

While the Westchester had no official logo, motifs such as this greeted passengers entering its stations. The Mercury caduceus, like this one at Quaker Ridge, was the most common. Author's photo, 1946.

An NYW&B Architecture Gallery ◉ 55

Columbus Avenue Junction in Mount Vernon was the Westchester's key operating point, and CA tower had to smoothly handle trains spaced an average of five minutes apart. Here a two-car express from Port Chester and New Rochelle comes through the junction slip switches. Immediately ahead of it was a White Plains local, which would meet this train at East Third Street station. George Votava photo, May 1937, Dave Keller archive.

4
RUNNING THE RAILROAD

The haste to get into operation was such that formal service hiccupped to a start in a succession of partial line openings. On May 29, 1912, trains started running between 180th Street and New Rochelle, essentially a useless service because New York-bound passengers had no direct connection to anything but local trolleys at 180th Street, unless they chose to hike several blocks west to the Bronx Park terminal of the IRT subway-elevated. Next, the White Plains Branch was opened July 5, but only as far as the outlying Mamaroneck Avenue station—and again, terminating at 180th Street at the south end. Service to the Westchester Avenue terminal came a month later, on August 10. In the meantime, on August 3, trains finally reached the Harlem River terminal, so by mid-August one could say that the full system was running. But even then, some stations, such as East 180th Street, were not finished (a temporary station was initially necessary), and one planned station in the southeast section of White Plains was not even definitively located. It is difficult to believe that many rode the Westchester during those first two months, but at least the railroad's operating employees had a chance to break in without too much pressure.[1]

Westchester president Leverett Miller and his schedule planners had been presented with a dilemma. It was all too clear that the Westchester's immediate traffic prospects were slim, and its territory would not need or support much more than a minimal service level. On the other hand, the service had to be frequent and attractive enough to develop the territory as quickly as possible and, not incidentally, comply with various franchise requirements. New York City insisted on at least 60 local trains a day, and Mount Vernon required 50 a day—almost a rapid transit operation. So while its neighboring suburban railroads had spent decades slowly building up their communities and traffic, the Westchester had to start off running full speed and stay that way, whether or not anyone was riding. (Admittedly, this was also true of new rapid transit lines in the Bronx, Brooklyn, and Queens, but these had other advantages, and their territories developed rapidly.)[2]

As one Westchester historian remarked, "The compromise reached was a bit extravagant—everyone got the best service."[3] During non-rush hours, trains ran on an unvarying 20-minute headway (that is, a train each way every 20 minutes) on both the New Rochelle and White Plains branches. The same 20-minute headway applied to both local and express services between the Harlem River and Mount Vernon, with expresses stopping only at Hunt's Point, East 180th Street, and Pelham Parkway in the Bronx and East Third Street in Mount Vernon. (Pelham Parkway was later dropped as an express station.)

Schedules were built around the Mount Vernon East Third Street express and local station and worked thusly: going north, for example, a local train would leave the Harlem River every 20 minutes, bound alternately for either New Rochelle or White Plains. An express departed 10 minutes later for whichever destination the local was not headed. The express caught up with the local at East Third Street, allowing an across-platform passenger interchange between the two. In that way, a passenger heading for New Rochelle who had boarded a White Plains train at some local stop then transferred to his New Rochelle train at East Third Street and was off with no time loss. At the same time, an express passenger wanting White Plains was also on his way. North of the Columbus Avenue junction, trains made local stops on each branch.[4]

Within several years it became clear that the New Rochelle Branch was generating most of the business, and this would become much more so in later years as the line was gradually extended to Port Chester. As a result, the schedule pattern was revised to favor this market, keeping the 20-minute base headway on both branches, but eliminating the alternating express trips to White Plains and New Rochelle. Instead, all expresses went to New Rochelle (and ultimately Port Chester) and all locals to White Plains. As before, East Third Street was the key transfer point, so passengers still had a virtually uninterrupted trip regardless of where they had boarded or where they were going and could count on such every 20 minutes. Except for the final bitter years, railroad maintained this 20-minute base headway and local-express pattern. Needless to say, its success demanded precise and punctual performance, and to its credit the Westchester almost always delivered. During August and September 1913, for example, 6,000 trains were operated with a 99 percent on-time record. (The only significant source of delay was the infrequently used drawbridge over the Bronx River at Westchester Avenue on the New Haven's Harlem River Branch.) Fred Kreschollek, who regularly rode the Westchester to school in the Bronx in the early 1930s, recalled, "In my lifetime I've traveled on many railroads, none of which could match the smoothness of the ride on the Boston Westchester. You could always depend on the accuracy of its timetables. The trains ALWAYS arrived on schedule."[5]

Making everything work smoothly put enormous pressure on the Columbus Avenue junction interlocking tower in Mount Vernon, which had to cope with an average of a train every five minutes and closer apart in rush hours. Its location less than a mile north of the East Third Street transfer station aggravated its problems, since all trains were scheduled to arrive and depart simultaneously at that point and pass through the junction within seconds of one another. Handling northbound services was especially frantic. Northbound local and express trains arrived and departed simultaneously at East Third Street, the White Plains train on the outside local track and the New Rochelle train on the inner express track. At the junction, the New Rochelle train had to enter its branch by crossing over from the center express track to the outside track in front of the approaching White Plains local. A smooth move was possible because the White Plains train made an intermediate stop at the Columbus Avenue local station just south of the junction. In the time it took it to slow, stop, and

The view looking south from CA tower as a northbound White Plains "train" negotiates the switches. The towerman has cleared a northbound New Rochelle–Port Chester train just moments earlier. Harry F. Brown photo, July 1924, author's collection.

accelerate out of that station, the New Rochelle train could overtake it and clear the junction without causing any delay. But the tower levermen had to scramble; they had 11.5 seconds to clear the circuit, change the switch lineup, and give a green signal to the White Plains train. This high-wire act was repeated over 50 times a day, with only rare delays.[6]

While the Westchester was a precisely timed operation, and while its trains could and did clip along at their 57 mph top speed on the long straightaways, overall terminal-to-terminal speed was somewhat more sedate. Expresses between the Harlem River and the East Third Street transfer station in Mount Vernon averaged about 32 mph; riding an express to East Third Street with local stops from there to White Plains took 40 minutes, for an average of 29 mph. In 1929, after the line reached its farthest terminal at Port Chester, overall terminal-to-terminal express-local running time to that point was 45 minutes—a slightly slower 28 mph average.[7] Even so, these running times were at least as good—and usually better—than comparable New Haven and New York Central schedules. But unfortunately, the total trip time into the city's center was another story, as will be noted shortly.

As part of the New Haven's "diversion" strategy (described in chapter 5), ticket prices were intentionally low relative to the New Haven and New York Central and remained that way. Throughout the Westchester's life, both its single-ticket and multiple-ride

A southbound Westchester car has just left the New Haven's Hunt's Point station on its exclusive trackage en route to the Harlem River terminal. The four-track NH Harlem River Branch is at its right. George Votava photo, December 1937, Dave Keller archive.

commutation rates were almost 40 percent below the Central's and New Haven's, and even factoring in the cost of the connecting nickel subway ride, they were more than 30 percent less. (And remember, many Grand Central passengers also had to ride the subway or streetcar.)[8]

In 1912 or 1913, the Westchester signed a contract with the Adams Express Company to handle small-package shipments over the line, presumably using the two passenger-baggage combines bought with the initial car order. In a promotional folder published shortly afterward, the company announced: "Four daily trains are operated over the line in both directions, carrying express matter only. Automobile trucks meet these trains and collections and deliveries are made with no delay whatever. A new system of express orders enables merchants and residents to place in the hands of the Express Company the purchase of goods and supplies in New York (or any center of trade). These orders are placed by telephone or by actual purchase through the organized agencies of the company and goods are in the hands of the consignee within a few hours." Little else is known about how this service operated, or for how long, but it seems doubtful that the daily "four trains in both directions" really carried "express matter only." Since the 54-seat combines probably handled the shipments, there was plenty of room for passengers, although the schedules may have been slower to accommodate loading and unloading work. Most likely, express shipments were handled only at the eight stations that were equipped to handle checked baggage and shipped corpses, that is, Harlem River, 180th Street, East Third Street Mount Vernon, Chester Heights, Wykagyl, Quaker Ridge, Heathcote, and the Westchester Avenue terminal at White Plains. Considering that the two combines were rebuilt to full coaches in 1922, it seems likely that the express-handling service was gone by that time. Afterward the railroad continued to handle checked baggage and corpses, although the tariff failed to specify how a corpse was to be carried on a regular coach.[9]

(Incidentally, this same promotional folder referred anyone interested in online real estate to the Millbrook Company at 37 Lawton Street in New Rochelle. The New Haven had kept the shell of the old Thorne-Perry company intact as a real estate broker and general NYW&B promoter, and it remained so until dissolved about 1917. While alive, the company also handled surplus bits of property bought during the line's construction.)

Morale was always high, and labor problems appear to have been few. There was never a strike or disturbance of any kind—a circumstance undoubtedly helped by the fact that, until the last grim days, there were no significant employee layoffs. Trainmen were decked out in smart uniforms different from their peers on the conventional steam railroads, and they were noted for their courtesy. In the line's early days they were given guidebooks to memorize in order to answer riders' questions about the railroad and its territory.[10] It was a first-class operation in all respects and remained so all its life.

As business built up, trains of up to five and six cars were run in rush hours. But off-peak traffic was another story: almost invariably, only single cars or at most two-car trains were needed at midday. In later years, after the New Rochelle Branch was extended to Mamaroneck and Port Chester, two cars often handled midday service on that line, but the lightly traveled White Plains Branch seldom saw more than one car "trains" most of the day. Despite frequent and highly reliable service, communities along that line simply did not develop very quickly.

The Westchester did acquire one high-toned neighbor in the southeastern section of White Plains when the Gedney Farm Hotel opened on Mamaroneck Avenue in 1914, close to its own recently opened Gedney Way station. Labeled by one Westchester County historian as "the pioneer Sun Valley," Gedney Farm was a sumptuous resort hotel, with swimming pool and adjacent golf club, tennis courts, garages, polo grounds, and stables. Luminaries such as Douglas Fairbanks and Mary Pickford, opera singer Mary Garden, Eddie Cantor, and the Guggenheim family were guests. It is unlikely that many of these patrons arrived on Westchester trains, but doubtless at least the help did. The hotel burned down in 1924 (there were no water lines out that far then to help save it), and its grounds were subsequently developed, with the golf course remaining. Although Gedney Farm perhaps brought some prestige to the Westchester's White Plains territory, its spacious facilities and resort-like surroundings also illustrated the lack of revenue-producing residential development there.[11] And in fact, the Westchester seemed to relish its rarified if underpopulated surroundings. In 1921, it published a promotional map specifically aimed at homebuyers who wanted to be near golf and yacht clubs, and there were 28 on or close to its lines at the time, with more to come.

From the beginning, though, the Westchester's primary problem was its New York terminals. For the railroad's first five years, passengers bound for anywhere in Manhattan had only one direct means of getting there: the IRT elevated shuttle at the Harlem

An all-too-typical single car service approaches the White Plains terminal, having just passed WP tower in the rear. George Votava photo, May 1937, Dave Keller archive.

Turning the other way, the photographer catches the train entering the Westchester Avenue terminal at White Plains. The NYW&B's small freight terminal is at the far left. George Votava photo, May 1937, Dave Keller archive.

River, a terminal site hardly in Grand Central's aesthetic league. The shuttle ran from the railroad terminal across the river to the 129th Street station of the Second and Third Avenue lines, where passengers had to transfer again. Even so, they were only delivered to the city's far east side, and they had to catch a crosstown streetcar to get elsewhere. Their only other choice was to walk several blocks to the IRT subway's 180th Street–Bronx Park terminal station—not a cheery prospect in bad weather.

This changed somewhat for the better as the New York subway system rapidly expanded under the 1913 "Dual Contracts." In March 1917, the IRT's White Plains Road subway extension was completed between East 177th Street and 238th Street, including the long-awaited express transfer station at East 180th Street adjacent to the Westchester's own 180th Street express station. The two were connected through a 300-foot enclosed passageway, and the 180th Street station quickly became the Westchester's busiest transfer point. Slightly more than a year later, the subway was rerouted from Fourth Avenue down to Seventh Avenue from Times Square, giving Westchester passengers direct rapid transit access to Manhattan's West Side. (Later, this line was tied to the new Lexington Avenue subway, allowing the riders two options.) A final subway connection came in January 1919 when the IRT completed its Lexington Avenue line to Hunt's Point, a block from the joint Westchester–New Haven station. (Another nearby station was opened in 1920 on the same line at Westchester Avenue.) Express subway service

The Westchester's Harlem River terminal facilities as they looked in 1937. The large building at the left, and its predecessor, served as the el transfer terminal until 1924, when a new station (at right) opened. The building also housed local New Haven freight and operating offices. George Votava photo, Bob's Photo collection.

In contrast, New York Central and New Haven commuters arrived here. The view dates to Grand Central's formal opening in 1913. Author's collection.

was available at both 180th Street and Hunt's Point and, starting in 1916, also on the two elevated lines at the 129th Street shuttle terminal.[12]

All of which was well and good, but time consumed by the subway or elevated transfers in the Bronx and the subsequent ride into the city center usually could not beat either the speed or aesthetic appeal of riding directly into Grand Central Terminal on the New Haven or New York Central. True, Grand Central passengers often also transferred to subways or streetcars to get to their final destinations, and the combination of NYW&B–subway running time to points in lower Manhattan such as Wall Street were almost competitive. But as the city's prime office and shopping districts gravitated to midtown, Grand Central's advantage became even greater. In many cases, commuters needed only to walk a few blocks, and some of that distance was even underground and out of the weather. Passengers may also have preferred Grand Central simply for psychological or social reasons: it was spacious, impressive, and always a con-

With the Triboro Bridge seen dimly in the background, a single southbound NYW&B car leaves the New Haven's Harlem River Branch on its way to its final stop. Although on New Haven property, the Westchester had its own segregated tracks. George Votava photo, November 1937, Dave Keller archive.

Inside a standard Westchester car as it awaits departure for White Plains in 1935. Up front, the motorman relaxes with his newspaper. Herman Rinke photo, author's collection.

A northbound White Plains car pauses at the Quaker Ridge station, amid idyllic suburban surroundings. Alfred Seibel photo, author's collection.

In another angle at Quaker Ridge, a southbound car leaves the center-island station. George Votava photo, December 1937, Bob's Photo collection.

Westchester freight operations typically looked like this. A northbound run with ten cars and a caboose crosses over at Columbus Avenue Junction on its way to White Plains. Freight service was confined to the Bronx, Mount Vernon, and the White Plains Branch; the New Rochelle–Port Chester line was exclusively passenger. George Votava photo, October 1937, Bob's Photo collection.

NYW&B freight facilities were humble and ignored by photographers. No operational photos seem to exist, but this 1951 view of the Heathcote freight house illustrates the basic style. The photo shows what was once the structure's track side, now used to provide truck access for its new owner. Note some catenary wire dangling forlornly above it. Author's photo.

Running the Railroad ◦ 67

venient place to meet, with dining and hotels next door. In contrast, the NYW&B always seemed to suffer from an image of terminal inferiority. In the view of Westchesterites, the Bronx had no class.

While the Westchester was conceived chiefly as a specialized passenger carrier, it did develop a modest interline freight business, particularly on the White Plains Branch. (Anything along the later Port Chester extension was the New Haven's turf.) Since the territory was almost entirely residential, it served few manufacturing businesses of any note and had little outbound traffic. Such business as existed was almost entirely inbound commodities consumed in suburban communities— coal for heating, building materials for new homes and roads, perishables and other foodstuffs, and miscellaneous manufactured goods. Typical of such customers was the Scarsdale Supply Company, the community's principal coal and building materials dealer, which was induced to relocate its storage yard to a site adjacent to the Westchester's Heathcote station in 1923.[13] By 1937, the freight customer list also included the Anheuser-Busch Brewing Company, the Lock Joint Pipe Company, Golden Brothers, and the Peckham Road Corporation, a building contractor. And in an era when coal was the primary heating fuel, several retail coal dealers had private sidings with unloading trestles. As part of its original construction, the railroad built a small freight yard and station at the west side of its Westchester Avenue terminal in White Plains that included team tracks and an unloading crane. Elsewhere, there were small freight stations for handling less-than-carload shipments at Mount Vernon (southeast of the East Sixth Street station), Heathcote, and Wykagyl. A public team track was also built at Gedney Way in White Plains to serve residential construction contractors in the area. But even at its peak, the Westchester's freight business brought in only about 5 or 6 percent of its total revenues and was easily handled by the railroad's one little jack-of-all-trades electric locomotive. (When it was occupied in other trades, such as work train duty, one of its New Haven sisters filled in.)[14] Most likely the company was just as happy to keep it that way. Although Miller had some creative ideas to expand the business, he always had to consider operational limits. More and heavier freight trains could well disrupt the dense, fast, and tightly scheduled passenger operations, not to mention adding the risk of such operational mishaps as derailments, broken couplers and air hoses, and the like.

So it was that the New York, Westchester & Boston became the first railway of its type in the United States to be scientifically designed and built new solely to handle high-volume suburban traffic in the most efficient possible manner. According to *Technical World,* a magazine of the *Popular Science* type, it was "the finest specimen of railroad building extant. In every detail, the [Westchester] measures up to the highest standard known to date."[15]

And well it should have, considering the price. As expected, the total bill for the railroad as completed in 1912 came high. Building and equipping the road alone had cost $22,344,165.07. Adding in $14,090,008.18 for miscellaneous real estate and all the elusive "intangibles" acquired before construction—such as stock, charters, franchises, and the like—the grand total came to $36,434,173.25 or, as the Interstate Commerce Commission later noted, "the remarkable per-mile cost of $2,020,752.81." Equated to 2006 dollars, that amounted to $760.5 million, or $42.2 million a mile—a huge sum by any standard.[16]

Tacitly acknowledging that the project was perhaps a peculiar business decision, the *Electric Railway Journal* nonetheless admired the result: "We prefer to recognize the courage, foresight, and belief of the builders in the future of New York and its suburbs, which were so great as to enable them to go ahead with a railway enterprise that is without parallel in this country."[17]

But exactly who was it that had such "courage, foresight, and belief" and had it in such quantity that no amount of money was too much to realize this dream?

Dethroned and deflated, an older and possibly wiser Charles Mellen sits alone in this undated photo, perhaps taken during the 1914 ICC hearings. He retired to his farm in Stockbridge, Massachusetts, and died in 1927 at age 75. Library of Congress, George G. Bain Collection, photo LC-B2-3633-14.

5
BUT WHY?

Thus far, this narrative has delicately sidestepped the glaringly obvious questions: Why was so much money poured into obtaining control of two questionable projects whose stock, as Charles Mellen later put it, "was not worth ten cents a pound" and whose tangible assets hardly matched the price paid? While the New Haven may have grossly overpaid for some of its steamship and streetcar companies, at least people could see, touch, and ride on the ships and trolleys. And why did acquiring these dubious assets demand such secrecy, subterfuge, and unsavory dealings? Once that was accomplished, why was it then decided to build what was essentially an unnecessary railroad to the highest possible engineering and construction standards—a railroad which, if successful, would only take business from its parent? And who ordered this?

Such questions were obvious even before the first shovelful of earth was turned. But the answers were elusive, and some of the most important remain so today. Official reasons were given, but they struck many knowledgeable observers as post-facto rationalizations.

It should be noted here that when the Westchester opened in 1912, nobody knew the story of how the New Haven first got involved and what happened next. Much of what was recounted in chapters 2 and 3 actually came to light later, the aftermath of a bitter series of events that culminated in the New Haven's near-bankruptcy and the humiliation of Charles Mellen.

It all started in 1907, when Mellen surreptitiously and illegally bought working control of the Boston & Maine, one of New England's three major rail systems and an important New Haven connection. The purchase aroused a storm of controversy in Boston, and one of the B&M's major stockholders, the Lawrence family, retained a local lawyer, Louis D. Brandeis, to take the New Haven to court. Up to then Brandeis had made an excellent living from his corporate law practice; in fact, he was a millionaire. Already, however, he was becoming more interested in public policy and the baneful political influence, monopolistic excesses, and general arrogance of powerful private interests such as those that Morgan and Mellen represented. Brandeis took on the case pro bono, but in order not to shortchange his law partners, he had his firm bill the Lawrences and then repaid them from his own pocket.[1]

Although his association with the Lawrences proved brief, the B&M case turned the naturally aggressive Brandeis into a full-time liberal crusader and a particular enemy of Mellen and the New Haven. Curious as to where Mellen was finding the money for all his profligate purchases, he began analyzing the company's reports and reading between the lines. In December 1907, he published a pamphlet bluntly accusing the New

Haven of fraudulent bookkeeping to conceal a rapidly deteriorating financial situation, complete with damning details. The pamphlet rocked New England, where the New Haven was considered on a par with the Bank of England and its stock was seen as the sustenance of widows and orphans. Needless to say, bankers, financiers, and the New Haven's kept press rushed to denounce Brandeis as an irresponsible, impudent, and unscrupulous amateur, and for the moment they had their day.[2]

But he spoke the truth, and soon there was trouble beyond Brandeis. In early 1911, railroad traffic had begun to drop off, and as the New Haven cut expenses drastically, its stock price dropped and rumors of a dividend cut began circulating. (By then, of course, the Westchester's construction was well under way, and nothing could be done about that.) Worse, thanks to maintenance and manpower cutbacks, employee morale went to pieces, creating a slack, don't-care attitude. During 1911, 66 passengers were killed and hundreds injured in a series of spectacular wrecks, and a once-worshipful public turned bitterly hostile.[3] (One of the classic lines in the record-setting 1947 play *Life with Father*, roughly set in this era, was this exchange: Clarence Day Jr. [reading the newspaper]: "Jiminy, another wreck on the New Haven. That always disturbs the stock market. Father won't like that." Vinnie: "I do so wish the New Haven would stop having wrecks. If they knew how it upsets your father.")

In 1913, everything began falling apart. Struggling to generate capital for new improvements (notably the Grand Central and Hell Gate Bridge projects) and increasingly short of cash, the New Haven already had bent state laws to allow it to take on more floating debt, while also reporting phantom dividends from subsidiaries to bolster its earnings. Brandeis, of course, made the most of this, demanding Mellen's resignation and a full federal investigation of the New Haven's financial affairs. Then, on March 31, 1913, J. P. Morgan, Mellen's patron saint and the New Haven's ruling power, died. Upon its founder's demise, J. P. Morgan & Company suddenly saw the light and threw its weight behind a stockholder committee that was fighting Mellen and his expansionist policies. Morgan's son, Jack, now in charge, had been disillusioned with Mellen for some time and was anxious to see him go. With his company crumbling and his backing gone, Mellen abdicated on July 17.[4] In December 1913, dogged by more wrecks and mounting financial troubles, the New Haven passed its dividend for the first time in 40 years.[5]

To replace Mellen, Jack Morgan brought in 54-year-old Howard Elliott, who had succeeded Mellen as president of the Northern Pacific. A native New Yorker, the Harvard-educated Elliott did his best to bring honesty to the New Haven's bookkeeping, austerity to its operations, and peace and hope to its workforce and the public. Before returning to the NP five years later, he managed to stabilize the situation and stave off bankruptcy. (Elliott did not abandon the New Haven entirely. Although he was president and chairman of the NP, his office was located in New York, and he remained a director of both the New Haven and Westchester.) But Elliott had to deal with the threat of a federal antitrust suit as well as stockholder lawsuits and possible criminal actions against Mellen and the directors, plus negotiating desperately for new financing and trying to fend off investigations and political attacks. Brandeis respected Elliott, but he continued to push for a full investigation into past sins and continuing "banker control" of the New Haven. He got his way, and on April 22, 1913, the Interstate Commerce Commission opened hearings in Boston, with the New York, Westchester & Boston affair a prime topic.[6]

Called on to explain the purchase, Mellen (who at the time was still the New Haven's president) said to ICC commissioner Charles Prouty:

> I am in a very embarrassing position, Mr. Commissioner, regarding the New York, Westchester and Boston. I have never been enthusiastic or at all optimistic of its being a good investment for our company in the present or immediate future. But people in whom I had greater confidence than I had in myself thought it was wise and desirable, and I yielded my judgment. Indeed, I do not know that it would have made much difference whether I yielded or not. . . .
>
> C. F. CHOATE [Mellen's lawyer]: Why should it stand the New Haven approximately $33 million?
>
> MELLEN: I wish I could give a better explanation. I do not know, really. I know that it did cost that, and I suppose and believe its cost was represented by the lawsuits, litigation, franchise values, giving away of capital stock, giving away of rights before we got hold of it; we simply had to pay through the nose to settle with everybody and everything, and it came near settling me.[7]

Here were the beginnings of the real story: the railroad's president forced by some unnamed higher authority, or authorities, to execute what he considered an unsound policy and apparently oblivious as to where the money went to pay for it. His implication was plain, though: there was no other god but Morgan, and Morgan decreed it.

The ICC's Boston investigation was relatively brief and, in the Westchester's case, did not probe too deeply; it simply concluded that the acquisition was another instance of buying out competition. But it turned out to be only a starter. Under pressure from Brandeis and the liberal senator George Norris, the ICC was persuaded to launch a more thorough investigation, which began August 14, 1914, under the ICC's new chief counsel, former Missouri governor Joseph Folk. Folk was known as a relentless prosecutor, and he took to the task with enthusiasm.[8]

Again, the Westchester's mysterious genesis was the central attraction. Mellen and Oakleigh Thorne were summoned from their respective retirements to shed what light they could. (His famously sarcastic wit still intact, the recently idled ex-president stated his occupation as "helping the Interstate Commerce Commission.") Between them they described the entire secret acquisition process already related here, beginning with Morgan's surprising creation of his "special committee" and the subsequent dealings with Thorne and Perry. The "hows" were thus mostly explained, although thanks to Mellen's memory and Thorne's incinerated records, the "whos" at the other end of the transactions were forever anonymous. Possibly for political reasons (it was a Democrat-inspired investigation, and Tammany Hall, of course, was Democratic), the ICC chose not to probe that subject further itself.

But more to the point was the "why?" Despite the voluminous testimony and exhibits, the ICC could not answer this, although it tried. The best that Mellen could offer was clearly only a partial and somewhat obvious answer. When Governor Folk said, "So the Westchester deal was simply buying up the possible competition from the Westchester line, is that so?" Mellen replied, "I think it would bear that construction."[9] It was equally clear from Mellen's and Thorne's testimony that the real reasons lay in J. P. Morgan's head, and J. P. Morgan had died the previous year.

In summarizing the Westchester affair, the ICC could only conclude, as it did in Boston, as follows:

> The Westchester is a story of profligate waste of corporate funds. The road was not necessary as a part of the New Haven system. . . .
>
> What could have been the motive for unloading the Westchester upon the New Haven at the expense of the stockholders of the latter must be left largely to conjecture. The only one accomplished result, however, of the Westchester transaction was the stifling of competition into New York City from New England.
>
> The blame for the Westchester rests squarely upon the directors of the New Haven road. Some are guilty for acts committed; others, the greater number, for their failure to act. They are all culpable and responsible to the stockholders.[10]

Kent T. Healy, professor of transportation at Yale University and earlier connected with the New Haven, believed that Morgan's optimism was a major reason for the Westchester acquisition and its lavish construction. Healy thought that Morgan sincerely believed that the territory it would serve offered tremendous potential and that building a high-capacity railroad from scratch would prove cheaper in the long run.[11] The professional trade magazine *Engineering News* agreed. In an editorial written shortly after the ICC investigation, the *News* said: "It is compatible with other New Haven exploits and other Morgan financings to believe that . . . the [New Haven] directors believed the [Westchester] properties would be worth the investment." But in summarizing, it echoed public opinion as well as the engineering profession's by pointing to the Westchester as a classic example of what happens when bankers run railroads.[12]

Although the Westchester was criticized as overly extravagant and, in hindsight, a profligate waste of resources, it also needs to be judged in the context of its time. The period before World War I was one of supreme optimism about rail traffic growth and, for some railroads such as the New Haven, enormous investment in high-capacity facilities to handle this business. Almost simultaneously, the New Haven was pumping large sums into its share of the new Grand Central Terminal, entirely rebuilding its Harlem River Branch, electrifying, and embarking on the hugely expensive Hell Gate Bridge project with the Pennsylvania Railroad. The Westchester was indeed costly and, in retrospect, undoubtedly a mistake, but its $36 million total price tag was a relatively small part of this picture. (Consider too that by the end of 1910 the Pennsylvania Railroad had spent $113 million on Penn Station and all its approaches and that the cost of Grand Central Terminal came to $80 million.)

Still, Morgan's direct and apparently decisive involvement in the Westchester episode has troubled Morgan biographers, some of whom have explained away this lapse of bankerly business judgment by putting all the blame on Mellen. Their general rationale has been that Morgan was old and otherwise preoccupied; he had left everything to Mellen, who was excessively enthusiastic about carrying out his master's wishes and who ultimately brought shame on Morgan's name.[13] That was true to a large extent. Morgan set policies, picked trusted men like Mellen and lawyer Francis Lynde Stetson to carry them out, and left the details to them. As an inborn empire-builder himself, Mellen did vastly overreach and overspend, albeit with Morgan's approval. But the Westchester did not seem to fit this pattern of leaving everything to the lieutenants, and the writers ignore Mellen's (mostly) credible testimony that he wanted nothing to do with the project. In his 1949 book, *The Great Pierpont Morgan,* Frederick Lewis Allen probably came closest to the truth. Morgan, he said, was always attracted to large, bold, and expensive ventures, and he usually had been successful with them. That, said Allen, led to some hubris and some flawed judgments in his old age. In the Westchester's specific case, "The idea of rounding out the New Haven system came as naturally as the idea of rounding out the Garland art collection; and if it cost a few extra millions, what did that matter?" In the end, though, for the New Haven's expansion in general and the Westchester in particular, "the irresistible force of Morgan's desire to do things in a big way . . . came face to face with immovable economic facts."[14]

So in the end, the biggest question remains frustratingly but everlastingly unanswered.

Beyond the Morgan conundrum, there were some practical questions about the Westchester project, particularly its route design. The railroad may have represented the epitome of railroad technology, but essentially it either went nowhere or duplicated established routes. To begin with, why did it end where it did? Its most fundamental weakness—its New York City terminals—was obvious from the beginning. To reach downtown, passengers had to transfer to the elevated at the Harlem River or, in subsequent years, the IRT subway-elevated lines at 180th Street and at Hunt's Point. True, if they used Grand Central, they still often had to use the subway to get to work, but doing so in the Bronx was less attractive than in midtown Manhattan, involving a longer and usually crowded ride. The low fares and superior service did entice riders, but the perception of "ending nowhere"—i.e., the Bronx—was a chronic handicap.

And speaking of nowhere, what was the point of the elaborately equipped White Plains Branch at all? As already noted, White Plains was never in New Haven territory, and it had been well served by the New York Central and its predecessor since 1844. Nor was there much of anything promising along the way to White Plains. The "major" intermediate points, such as Heathcote, Quaker Ridge, and Wykagyl, then sat in a population desert, although theoretically they had promising development potential.

The answers to those two questions were quickly forthcoming and seemed superficially plausible. The Bronx terminals were intended as such, the railroad said, to divert suburban traffic from Grand Central Terminal, then being built. While the New Haven had almost perpetual rights to enter the station, it paid for them—first, to use New York Central tracks between Grand Central and Woodlawn and, second, to use the station itself, for which it paid a per-passenger fee. In 1906 that fee was 18 cents a head, which was raised to 24 cents in 1912 in anticipation of the new terminal's completion. The total cost was not overly burdensome for long-distance traffic, but it was lethal for the short-haul, low-revenue commuter business. In fact, the commuter ticket price from such nearby cities as Mount Vernon and New Rochelle just about equaled the terminal charges, leaving aside any train operation or overhead costs. It was obvious, too, that this unprofitable business would greatly increase in the coming years, making a miserable situation intolerable. The solution, Mellen stated, was to lure some of this business to transfer stations in the Bronx by giving them a more attractive service at a lower price. He admitted that the project probably would never pay for itself, but in a burst of magnanimity he declared, "The Westchester commuters are served by a broad-minded corporation which is giving them more than they had heart to ask."[15]

To many perceptive observers, all that smacked of justifications conjured up after the decisions were made. A quick glance at the New Haven's map showed that the Westchester was completely unnecessary for that purpose. Excepting the Westchester's admittedly important 180th Street transfer station, the new railroad simply shared the New Haven's right-of-way to the already existing New Haven Harlem River terminal, using two dedicated tracks of its own. The New Haven could have offered direct service between Port Chester, New Rochelle, and the Harlem River on its own tracks. (In fact, as described earlier, it had been running frequent suburban trains between New Rochelle and the Harlem River for many years, and did so in diminishing form until 1930.) And serving the 180th Street subway connection could easily be accomplished by building a short loop or branch off the New Haven line—only a quarter of a mile away at this point—at relatively low cost.

But following the diversion rationale, there speculatively might have been another motive that made long-term sense. Even in the early 1900s, both the New Haven and New York Central had no illusions about the profitability of their commuter business. But they were stuck with it, and given the nature of their clientele, it was smart to show the best possible corporate face. So as long as they were making good profits elsewhere, they could afford this expensive form of public relations. The Westchester, however, was technically an independent company that, if official statements were to be believed, was formed primarily to siphon off the New Haven's commuters. In the future, if the New Haven ever chose to do so, it could divorce itself from the Westchester and be free (or at least freer) of its suburban service obligations.

As a justification for the remote Harlem River terminal, some later historians have argued that the New Haven–Westchester planners had anticipated that New York City's commercial center would continue to move northward to 125th Street, making the terminal more convenient. And, they continue, had it not been for a 1916 zoning ordnance that stopped major commercial development at 59th Street, perhaps this would have happened. Maybe it would have, maybe not, but in any event, neither the New Haven nor the Westchester managements ever mentioned this in their various justifications. And even had there been no such zoning law, given the normal northward pace of commercial development in Manhattan, it would have been decades before anything significant reached that far—if it ever did.

As for the White Plains Branch, Mellen explained that the New Haven was planning a line called the Westchester Northern, which would extend from White Plains northward to connect with key east-west and north-south New Haven freight routes. This was to form a valuable direct freight and passenger link to the Berkshires and western New York State and also interchange freight links to Pennsylvania and western points. So in time, the White Plains line would assume far more importance than merely as a commuter route. More will be said on that immediately.

The proposed route of the Westchester Northern, c. 1910. © Otto M. Vondrak.

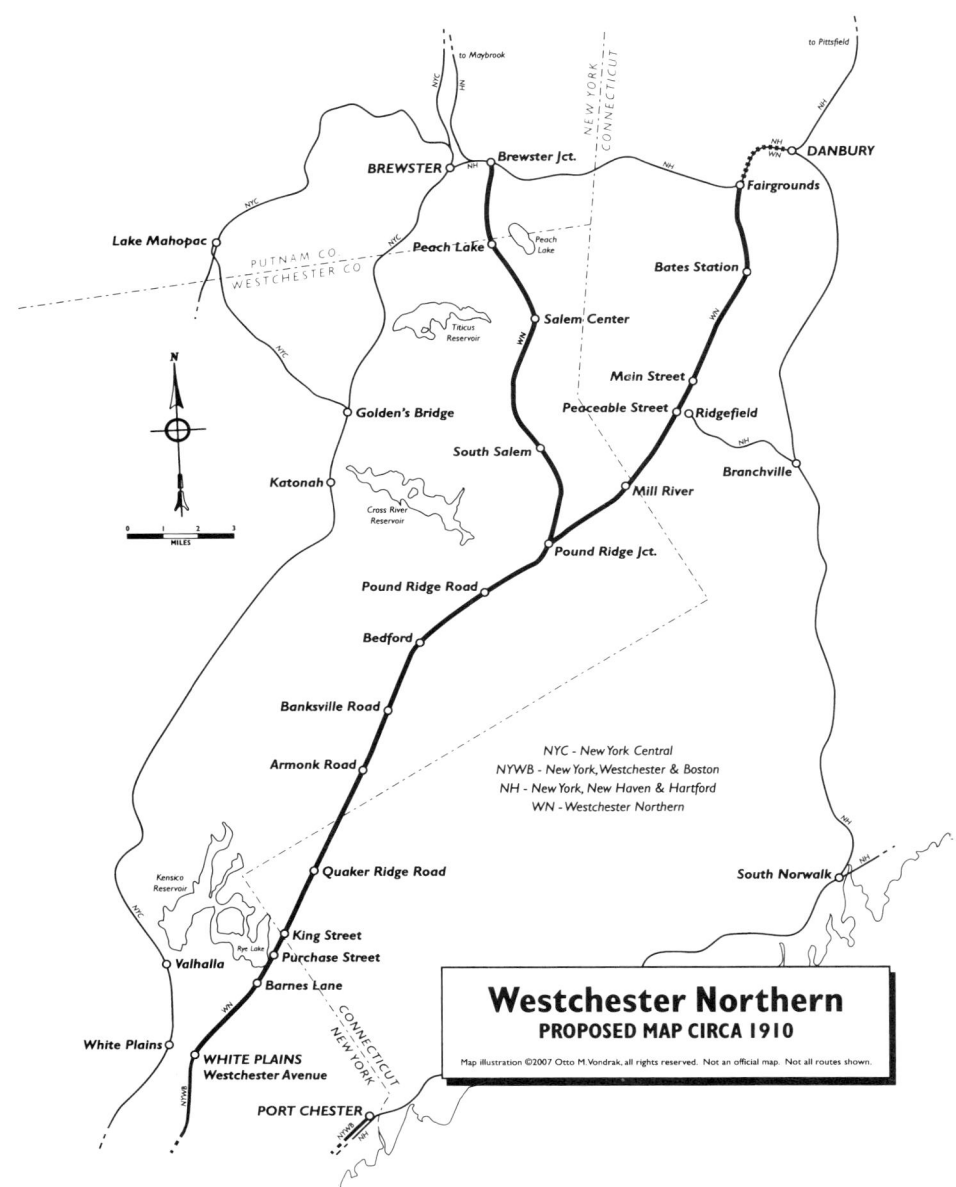

6

THE PHANTOM WESTCHESTER NORTHERN

Actually, the question of "Why build the White Plains Branch?" seemed to have two answers, one well publicized, the other not. The lesser-noted one was straightforward enough: it simply *had* to be built. The New York State Public Service Commission required it as part of the full NYW&B system. That made it a classic, if rather overbuilt, developmental line, meant to open a new suburban territory considered too remote from neighboring railroads to be attractive, especially in an era when automobiles were still few and roads poor. (And in that sense it was much like the past and future elevated and subway lines built into the farmlands of the Bronx, Brooklyn, and Queens.) But the New Haven had also previously come up with its own justification, which it announced in 1912: the White Plains Branch was to be the key link in an ambitious project that would create new, more direct freight routes between New York and New England and between New York and western points.

Parts of that story remain an undocumented puzzle to present-day historians. But the idea had first appeared back when Thorne and Perry's Millbrook Company was gathering up all the corporate pieces that would be turned over to the New Haven to form its "new" New York, Westchester & Boston. On October 1, 1907, Thorne and Perry incorporated a mysterious company called the Mount Vernon & Eastern Railroad, which would build northeast to Danbury, Connecticut, where it would join other New Haven lines. The MtV&E became a Millbrook subsidiary, but it did nothing concrete and was finally dissolved in 1911. Whatever assets it owned were turned over to the NYW&B's Leverett Miller, who was noted as a MtV&E stockholder at that time.[1]

In the meantime, the MtV&E plan had changed corporate form. On February 8, 1910, a month after the NYW&B's merger and reincorporation as a New Haven satellite, Leverett Miller, along with the Westchester's auditor and lawyer, filed incorporation papers for the Westchester Northern Railroad. This line was clearly a replacement for the MtV&E and was to form an extension of the NYW&B from White Plains to both Danbury, Connecticut, and Brewster, New York. Its route would proceed from White Plains northward through North Castle, nick the western corner of Greenwich, Connecticut, and then return to Westchester County. At Pound Ridge, in Westchester, the line was to split, with branches heading in a "Y" pattern northeast to Danbury, via

Ridgefield (almost exactly following the MtV&E route) and northwest to Brewster, passing through Bedford and North Salem. For some arcane corporate reason, the Westchester Northern initially was wholly owned by the City and County Contract Company, a construction affiliate of the 1904 NYW&B company that was set up by its promoters to help enrich themselves. It had come to the New Haven along with Mellen's "not worth ten cents a pound" Westchester securities.[2]

At both terminals, the Westchester Northern would join the New Haven's so-called Maybrook Line, its strategic freight route connecting the mainline west of New Haven with important interline connections at Maybrook, New York, via the Hudson River bridge at Poughkeepsie. The Brewster leg would form a New York shortcut for freight interchanged between the New Haven and four eastern railroads at Maybrook. At Danbury, the Westchester Northern would meet New Haven's Berkshire Division, which followed the Housatonic River north through western Connecticut and New York State, ending at Pittsfield, Massachusetts. It also joined the eastern portion of the Maybrook Line, which led east to Devon and the New Haven's key Cedar Hill classification yard at New Haven, Connecticut.

Traffic between the Berkshire line and New York traditionally followed one of two routes: a direct line south to the mainline at South Norwalk, Connecticut, or a more circuitous routing to the east through Botsford and Bridgeport. Most New York passenger trains used the South Norwalk line; the Botsford–Bridgeport route bypassed Danbury and carried some through passenger trains as well as increasing freight traffic, some of which was routed over this line to avoid conflicts with passenger trains on the South Norwalk line.[3]

In theory, Westchester Northern connections at Danbury and Brewster could channel large amounts of freight to and from New York. The Brewster–Maybrook route potentially offered anthracite coal and cement from eastern Pennsylvania, as well as refrigerator traffic and merchandise shipments moving through interline routes connecting into the Midwest and West. (It is unclear, however, how much coal actually would come into New York over this route, since most of the anthracite-oriented lines that fed into Maybrook had their own coal transfer facilities on the New Jersey side of New York Harbor.) The Berkshire Division through Danbury handled a reasonably heavy freight business, including substantial traffic interchanged with the New York Central's Boston & Albany subsidiary at State Line, New York. A Westchester Northern–NYW&B route would give this freight a more direct path into New York, removing it from the New Haven's always congested mainline. The Westchester Northern's Danbury connections also provided an alternate route for moving freight between points east of Cedar Hill (such as Boston and Providence) and New York, further relieving the New Haven mainline along the Sound shore. In addition, at about this time or shortly thereafter, the New Haven toyed with the idea of making the Berkshire line part of a new New York–Montreal route, which would have fed considerably more traffic. Berkshire Division passenger traffic was less dense but included a substantial milk business.

Freight traveling over both Westchester Northern branches would use NYW&B tracks from White Plains to the New Haven's Oak Point yard in the Bronx; there it would either move by carfloat to connections and customers around New York Harbor or, in the future, travel the planned Hell Gate Bridge route through Queens and Brooklyn to another carfloat transfer terminal at Bay Ridge. The New Haven also apparently planned to route some of its Berkshire Division passenger trains over the Westchester Northern–NYW&B route and thence into Grand Central through a new connection at Mount Vernon. The Hell Gate Bridge route into Penn Station was an alternative that would require no additional construction work.

Whether the Westchester Northern eventually was to be electrified is uncertain, but initially it was to be steam-operated. (However, it was generally carried in railway directories as an electric railroad.) Since the anticipated traffic would be primarily freight, electrification would have been unnecessary, as the trains would avoid those areas in New York where steam was technically prohibited. But any passenger trains moving between the Berkshire Division and either Grand Central or Penn Station would need electric power, so a changeover facility and engine house would be needed at some location, most likely White Plains. Since there was no space at or near the NYW&B's White Plains terminal, this probably would have been located somewhere in the more rural areas just north of the city. (Faced with the same problem, the New York Central built its engine-change facilities and yard at North White Plains.)

Shortly after the company's incorporation in 1910, the Millbrook Company (which was still an active New Haven subsidiary, now in the real estate business) bought some property along the route. How much, and where, is a mystery, although it was estimated that one-third of the route was acquired. A 1937 NYW&B property tax analysis still showed parcels scattered along the line, the largest being at North Castle, New York, and at Greenwich and Ridgefield, Connecticut. (One parcel in Greenwich eventually reverted to the estate of its original owner and ended up being known as Yale Farms after being donated to Yale University.) Evidence of smaller bits of property showed up at Bedford, Lewisboro, and Pound Ridge, New York, as well as at Danbury. Aside from a small parcel at Bedford, there seems to be no surviving evidence of real estate activity along the Brewster Branch, which appeared to be an afterthought anyway.[4]

With so many other things happening in 1910 and 1911—most of them bad—the New Haven was slow to do anything more about the idea. Aside from the Millbrook Company's early property purchases, little was done until shortly after the NYW&B itself was completed. Then, in October 1912, the New Haven directors authorized the railroad's construction, estimated at between $6 and $7 million. Immediately afterward, $2 million worth of NYW&B bonds reportedly were sold to cover the initial part of the work. (These bonds were part of the same issue that financed the Westchester's construction.) The same report mentioned that construction was to start in early November. What was actually done, if anything, is yet another unknown; some accounts mention grading work, but the usually authoritative *Poor's Railroad Manual* flatly stated five years later that there had been no construction.[5] In any event, the project's most visible landmark was the odd steelwork on the roof of the Westchester's White Plains terminal building, as well as extra-heavy steel internal framing. All this was to support Westchester Northern passenger trains, which were to use new upper-level platforms atop the NYW&B tracks and be carried over Westchester Avenue in front of the station on a girder bridge. (The planners may or may not have envisioned a separate alignment for freights; if they did, nothing was started for it.) Also, at some unknown date—probably during the NYW&B's construction—work was begun on a connecting ramp where the Westchester crossed over the New Haven's mainline at Columbus Avenue in Mount

The NYW&B's White Plains terminal at Westchester Avenue, as it looked in 1912. Note the steel structure on the roof, designed to carry an upper deck for Westchester Northern trains. Robert A. Bang collection.

Vernon, for use by New York–Pittsfield passenger trains heading to or from Grand Central.

As the New Haven stumbled toward financial disaster in 1913, it hardly needed an expensive new railroad-building project, and the Westchester Northern dropped into limbo—alive but out of the question for the time being. It had never reached the point of obtaining franchises from any municipality along the way, and if any construction had actually been started, it was not much. The Westchester's balance sheet as of June 30, 1913, showed that the company had spent $7,825 on the project up to that time, but what that represented—whether advances to Millbrook for WN real estate or WN-related work on its own property—is uncertain, too.[6]

As part of Howard Elliott's efforts to clean up Mellen's messes, the Westchester formally absorbed the moribund Westchester Northern on June 1, 1915, probably signaling its death at that time. By the early 1920s, the Westchester was concentrating what resources it had on its Port Chester extension, and it had officially filed with the New York State Public Service Commission to abandon the enterprise. Permission came in May 1925, and the Westchester Northern was finally dead, with the funds held aside for it used to push the Port Chester line east from Larchmont. Part of its route finally came to life 43 years later as a section of Interstate 684.

It was probably just as well. How a Westchester Northern–NYW&B route would have worked is an open question. A reasonably heavy freight volume would have been necessary to economically justify building such a line, but how was it to be handled? Doing so in daytime hours would have been difficult, if not impossible. Rush hours aside, passenger trains between White Plains and Mount Vernon were scheduled every 20 minutes each way all day and into the early evening; between Mount Vernon and the Harlem River, the headway averaged 10 minutes. (And as mentioned earlier, the key Columbus Avenue junction in Mount Vernon was faced with routing trains through its interlocking on an average of every 5 minutes. Operators in the New Haven's Oak Point interlocking would have been equally harried, and doubtless also would be offering daily prayers that there would be no broken coupler knuckles or parted air hoses while crossing over six tracks of two busy main lines.) The only practical operating period would have been after about 2 a.m., when there was more than a three-hour clear window when no passenger trains were scheduled on the White Plains Branch and only hourly service on the New Rochelle line. But even so, precise crew and train operation would be required so that everything was out of the way before the morning rush hour.

The Westchester's minimal once-a-day local freight to White Plains was one thing, but adding in long, lumbering freight trains (and especially coal drags) was emphatically another and not a match made in heaven. The Westchester was justly proud of its precise scheduling and on-time performance. It was equally proud of its first-class track condition, which such freights would not be kind to. The route looked nice on a map, but operating it south of White Plains would have been a nightmare. Nor would the Westchester's upper-class suburbanites have been happy about steam-powered freights rattling past their homes and gardens, especially in the middle of the night.

Unfortunately, the Westchester Northern remains one of the more opaque of the Westchester's several mysteries. Deeper research is needed, assuming some enlightening documentation still exists. Until then, questions abound: Was the Westchester's White Plains Branch originally planned with this extension in mind, or was the Westchester Northern conjured up after the basic decisions were made? While construction cost estimates apparently were made, what revenues and operating costs were assumed? Did the New Haven ever actually get into the detailed operational and traffic-flow planning that would have addressed such questions as what kinds of traffic the line would handle, what extra facilities would be needed, how train operations were to be meshed with Westchester schedules, and how passenger trains would be routed and where they would change power? Given the timing, how serious could the New Haven's board have been in 1912 when it authorized construction? By then their railroad's deteriorating finances were becoming plain, even without Brandeis's help. Operating and maintenance costs were being cut frantically, while funds had to be found for large commitments such as the Hell Gate project. Did the board really want to spend their railroad's rapidly draining resources for what was more a convenience than a necessity?

There is also the intriguing puzzle of whether the New Haven's interest in the project actually dated to a short time before the Mount Vernon & Eastern was organized in 1907, when the ghost of a partially completed late nineteenth-century New York–Danbury railroad appeared. Few facts about this earlier company are known, but what can be pieced together runs like this:

As mentioned in chapter 1, after the Civil War, a variety of railroad entrepreneurs were scrambling to put together rail lines between New York and Boston. At least by 1870, a three-railroad combination (two of which merged as the New York, New Haven & Hartford in 1872) was operating through New York–Boston trains via New Haven, Hartford, and Springfield, Massachusetts.[7] Another chain of railroads had been built along the shore line between New Haven and Boston via Providence and formed an alternate route that eventually would become the New Haven's main line.

There always seemed to be more opportunity, though, and several companies were hatched to build another "inside route" to compete with the evolving New Haven system. Our own original New York, Westchester & Boston was probably one, although it never got as far as obtaining a charter beyond New York State. Earlier, another company, the New York, Housatonic & Northern, started toward New York from the opposite direction. Chartered in 1864, the NYH&N planned to build from Brookfield, Connecticut, to Danbury and thence through western Connecticut and Westchester County to White Plains. There it was to connect with the New York & Harlem, which it would use to enter New York. The NYH&N completed its line between Brookfield and Danbury in 1868 and reportedly graded 23 miles of its roughly 30-mile route between Danbury and White Plains, some of which is still visible. But in 1871 it changed its plan to join the Harlem at White Plains and created a company called the Southern Westchester, which would build an independent line between White Plains and an elaborate terminal station at the Harlem River. (Speculatively, this move may have been forced by Commodore Vanderbilt's integration of the New York & Harlem with his newly merged New York Central & Hudson River Railroad and the subsequent completion of his grandiose Grand Central Depot on the Harlem's right-of-way in 1871 to serve his entire rail system. The result may have been that, for whatever reason, the NYH&N could not use the Harlem into New York, and thus found itself marooned at White Plains.) The Southern Westchester acquired property in Mount Vernon at what is now Willson's Woods Park and reportedly did some construction there as well as elsewhere south of White Plains, but no record of it now remains.

With the Southern Westchester's formation, a joint Southern Westchester–NYH&N route was to form a wholly independent link between New York, Danbury, and Brookfield. At Brookfield it would connect with the Housatonic Railroad (later the New Haven's Berkshire Division) for points north into western Massachusetts and, more important, at Danbury with the then-unfinished Boston, Hartford & Erie (later New York & New England) leading to Hartford and Boston. The Southern Westchester and NYH&N merged in September 1872 under the NYH&N name, but the combination collapsed in late 1874 and was foreclosed the following year. Its assets were sold in 1881. The 1874 merger may have been precipitated by financial problems, because in that year creditors leased the completed Brookfield–Danbury section to the Housatonic Railroad, which used it as its entry to Danbury and which finally purchased that segment from the defunct company in 1882.

The story then melts into another fog, but in July 1906 C. E. Arnold, a vice president of a shadowy company called the New York, Boston, Albany & Schenectady Railroad, approached the New Haven and offered to sell it the partially graded New York–Danbury line. Judging by the company's rather diffuse name, it may have been intended as a blackmail strike indiscriminately aimed at either the New York Central or New Haven, presumably following the same route as the Westchester Northern and branching to form routes to Danbury and to Albany. Presumably, too, it had somehow acquired the old New York, Housatonic & Northern–Southern Westchester rights-of-way. There was no sale, but it may not have been coincidental that the Mount Vernon & Eastern appeared a year later under the suspected aegis of the New Haven. So perhaps this nineteenth-century phantom may have inspired the railroad to conjure its own second phantom.[8]

Photos of the NYW&B's 1924 Harlem River terminal are at the hen's teeth level of scarcity. In this 1939 view west of Willis Avenue, new IRT "World's Fair" subway cars are being delivered over the old el spur connecting with the New Haven. The Westchester terminal building shows up at the far right, together with the covered walkway to the Third Avenue el's 133rd Street station. In the rear is an el train entering its station. Joseph Testagrose collection.

7

MAKING THE BEST OF LIFE, 1913–1929

Leaving behind it the sorry (but spicy) tale of its high-born paternity, the New York, Westchester & Boston moved on to its job of being an exemplary suburban servant—quiet, efficient, reliable, and perhaps a bit dull. There were, of course, the inevitable growing pains. Its maiden annual statement, covering the fiscal year ending June 30, 1913, reported an impressive $1.4 million deficit on revenues of a meager $289,000. Even on the narrower basis of operating ratio, its performance was breathtakingly bad. (Operating ratio is the percentage of pure day-to-day operating expenses to operating revenues, omitting such items as bond interest, taxes, and other fixed expenses. The lower the figure the better, and anything above 80 or so indicates trouble. The Westchester's 1912–1913 operating ratio came in at 162.) Westchester president Leverett Miller hastened to explain what was obvious anyway: that this dismal first-year performance was expected and could be attributed to sparse development in the line's territory and the lack of adequate rapid transit connections in the Bronx. As yet, he noted, the subway had not been extended to the 180th Street transfer station, and all that existed was the inconvenient double transfer via the elevated shuttle at the Harlem River. Once the proper facilities were completed, he continued, the Westchester would be able to meet its operating expenses, probably by 1919 or 1920. By then, too, he predicted, its territory would be developing and income would rise steadily.[1]

And things did quickly improve, at least relatively so. Although the 1914 deficit was $1.5 million, revenues already had improved by almost 40 percent, and operating expenses were 8 percent less. Thanks to its efficient design and operation, plus its brand-new plant and equipment, the operating ratio dropped to a more reasonable 84 by 1914–1915 and steadily improved afterward. This meant that the railroad was covering its direct operating expenses by 1915, but not yet its taxes. By 1929, with the system complete and traffic at its peak, the ratio was a very commendable 64, considerably below most large steam railroads. In fact, through virtually all of its life—including the unhappy Depression years—the Westchester always covered its direct operating expenses, if nothing more. From the perspective of present-day publicly operated rapid transit and suburban rail services, such performance is virtually unheard of. Revenues inevitably rose. Within two years of the line's opening—and before the 180th Street subway connection was opened—operating income had risen over 56 percent. With all subway connections finally in place, the 1919–1920 operating revenues totaled $912,265, a hair short of $1 million and 216 percent above that raggedy first year.

The killers, of course, were the fixed expenses: interest on the railroad's high construction debt, the inevitable property taxes (which in turn were based on the railroad's extravagant construction), and rentals to the New Haven for track and facilities use. These ranged from about $1.4 million in the early years to over $2.5 million when the last line extension was completed in 1929. Never could the Westchester entirely cover them (although it partially did so in 1929), and bond interest went unpaid from the beginning until the end. Beset by its own financial problems but committed to its guarantee, the New Haven sullenly covered it, throwing it back onto the Westchester's balance sheet as accumulated debt. Possibly the Westchester's beleaguered parent secretly hoped that the Brandeis-inspired federal antitrust suit against it would force divesture, but sadly, no. The Justice Department's 1914 settlement did require the New Haven to put its Boston & Maine stock in trusteeship and sell its steamship and trolley companies, but the government generously let the New Haven keep its prodigal child, considering it just a part of the parent's suburban operations.[2]

Nonetheless, things steadily brightened over the next 15 years. Although never wholly satisfactory, the New York terminal connections were improved, traffic multiplied, net operating earnings increased, some physical improvements were made, the promised Port Chester extension was completed, and the railroad steadily enticed more New Haven riders with its more frequent service and lower fares. There was one very noticeable difference, though: all new structures were built at the lowest cost necessary to accommodate the business.

First to be taken care of were the Bronx rapid transit connections. As noted, when the Westchester opened in 1912, its only Manhattan link was the elevated at the Harlem River. This consisted of a one-stop shuttle from the railroad terminal to 129th Street in upper Manhattan, where Westchester passengers transferred again to the Second or Third Avenue elevated lines. After 1916, both ran express trains from 129th Street, but the double transfer still was a nuisance, and many passengers needed a third transfer to get to work or to stores, since they were landed on the east side of the city.

Some relief came in 1917 when the Interborough Rapid Transit extended its subway-elevated branch north beyond its Bronx Park terminal, establishing an express station at 180th Street only 300 feet from the Westchester's 180th Street express stop and linked through an enclosed passageway. Initial service began March 3, when IRT trains began running on its new White Plains Road Branch as far as 219th Street; full operation to 238th Street followed on March 31. (In 1920 the line was further extended to its present terminal at 241st Street.)[3] Once in place, the 180th Street facility became the line's busiest transfer point; from there passengers could use either the Lexington Avenue subway or, with a same-platform transfer, the Broadway line (which in 1918 became Broadway–Seventh Avenue). A final downtown link arrived January 8, 1919, when the IRT completed its Lexington Avenue subway-elevated to Hunt's Point Avenue, where it built an express station near the Westchester's own express stop at the grandiose New Haven station.

Ahead of the anticipated traffic growth, the Westchester added 10 more multiple-unit motor cars and five identical trailers in 1915, bringing its roster up to 45 cars. (The trailers turned out to be a case of overanticipating. To maintain the Westchester's fast schedules, they could only be used in a ratio of four motor cars per trailer. While the railroad did run five-car rush hour trains, they did not run enough, and the underutilized trailers were given motors in 1928.)[4]

Next, the Harlem River situation was slightly improved when it was decided to replace the elevated shuttle to 129th Street with a relocated railroad terminal that would be closer to the Third Avenue el's 133rd Street express station. For passengers, that meant a 400-foot hike through a partially enclosed elevated passageway (and en route negotiating up-and-down ramps with 10 percent grades to hurdle the IRT's el yard underneath), but at least it saved one transfer. Construction started in September 1923, and the new terminal opened the next year on April 15. Located on a steel trestle west of the old facilities and Willis Avenue, it typified the Westchester's new era of frugality. Instead of a Mediterranean villa with concrete platforms adorned with Doric columns, Westchester riders detrained onto utilitarian wood platforms and passed through an austere, single-story square brick building that they barely noticed.[5]

Although the New Haven was still financially anemic following the war—and still not paying dividends—it recognized that it must put more money into its offspring. With its mainline truncated at New Rochelle and the Westchester Northern project probably doomed to oblivion, the Westchester was not serving its intended purpose. It was beginning to siphon off some New Haven business at New Rochelle, Pelham, and Mount Vernon, but not yet enough to justify itself. So with the war over and the promise of economic growth returning, the New Haven decided to carry through its publicly stated "Grand Central diversion" strategy and push the line onward toward Port Chester as its original charter specified while keeping it physically separate from its parent.

Where to place the Westchester line evidently went through a change of plan, however. As can best be deduced now, the earliest thinking apparently envisioned crossing the New Haven's mainline a short distance from the Westchester's North Avenue station and then following the route originally proposed by the 1904 NYW&B promoters, which lay on its own right-of-way just to the New Haven's east. To this end, at about the

An outbound Port Chester train leaves the 1924 Harlem River terminal, passing the old platforms on the left. George Votava photo, October 1937, Bob's Photo collection.

Making the Best of Life • 89

A northbound five-car rush hour express crosses Allerton Avenue in the Bronx, bound for New Rochelle. George Votava photo, December 1937, Dave Keller archive.

time the original line to New Rochelle was built in 1911–1912, the New Haven constructed a substantial concrete interlocking tower at Larchmont Junction, the point west of the NYW&B's North Avenue station where its line joined the parent and originally had a track connection.

But by 1920, economy and pragmatism prevailed. The New Haven's four-track main-line right-of-way already had space for two additional tracks, and its station buildings at Larchmont, Mamaroneck, Harrison, and Rye could be jointly used, making for a minimal cost. One alternative was to use the same projected crossing at Larchmont Junction but follow the east side of the New Haven line to Port Chester. This would save the expense of relocating the existing New Haven stations—all of which were located on the west side of the tracks—as well as allowing unhindered access to its Mamaroneck freight yard, also west of the mainline. Nonetheless, in the end it was decided to build along the New Haven's west side, jack up the four New Haven stations and move them west to accommodate, and cross the Mamaroneck yard lead track at grade.

The Port Chester extension job was done in four short hops spread over 10 years, carried on as money permitted and as patronage built. Grading and laying track as far as Larchmont, about 1.3 miles began in 1920 and opened to a station at Chatsworth Avenue in Larchmont in March 1921. (In the process, the almost-new Larchmont Junction tower was demolished, the track connection was removed, and Larchmont Junction itself ceased to exist.) The Larchmont extension's $418,500 total cost was low indeed. Deflated back to 1912 dollars, that worked out to about $151,300 a mile, which was 85 percent below the original line's per-mile construction cost.[6] One intermediate Westchester-only station was built at Pine Brook in New Rochelle and was the very definition of frugality—little more than a bare little wood box at the bottom of an overpass stairway, leading out to a single center wood platform and overhead canopy.

After a lull of several years, the extension was on the move again. On March 26, 1926, Westchester trains began running as far as Mamaroneck, 1.5 miles beyond Larchmont,

Larchmont Junction in New Rochelle, as it looked in 1913 soon after the NYW&B was opened as far as New Rochelle. The view looks east, with the New Haven mainline on the right. Note the New Haven tower in the left rear, built to control a planned NYW&B–NH crossing for the future Port Chester extension, which would have paralleled the NH to its east. Harry F. Brown photo, author's collection.

Approximately the same spot as it looked after the Larchmont extension was finished, with the tower gone and the NYW&B located on the west side of the NH mainline. George Votava photo, November 1937, Dave Keller archive.

Making the Best of Life ○ 91

Just east of the onetime Larchmont Junction, an eastbound train skirts the NH mainline on the right. Ed Hurmanns photo, October 1937, Dave Keller archive.

serving another new station of their own at Larchmont Gardens on the way. Larchmont Gardens continued the austerity mode, but the modest single-story brick structure was at least a step up from the minimal Pine Brook facility. Another short step to the New Haven station at Harrison was completed July 3, 1927, with a new stop about midway at West Street, Harrison.

Rye came next in the summer of 1928, and on December 8, 1929, the electric cars first rolled into the terminal at Port Chester.[7] (In keeping with the New Haven's apparent intent to keep the two railroads at arm's length, there was no connection between the tracks anywhere along the route, even though the tracks were immediately adjacent and four stations were jointly used.) At Port Chester, the NYW&B built its own station across the street from the New Haven's station along with a severely unpretentious interlocking tower and a storage yard to its south. But unlike its other structures on the New Rochelle–Port Chester extension, the Westchester's one-story terminal station was a relatively large brick building with a slight bit of architectural flair, including large arched windows with simplified fan lights and a tile roof.

In all, the Port Chester extension added 8 miles to the Westchester system, giving it a total of 30 route miles, about 12 of which were on New Haven property.

As the Westchester worked its way toward Port Chester, more cars were bought to handle its growing business, although in this case the Westchester was not the buyer. With no borrowing power of its own, it had to rely on the New Haven's somewhat better resources, and so the parent paid for and owned all subsequent equipment. Ten new cars came in 1924, 20 more in 1926, and 20 in 1927, giving the Westchester a grand total

The NYW&B's Pine Brook station in New Rochelle was economy personified. The New Haven's mainline is in the foreground. George Votava, November 1937, Bob's Photo collection.

Work is still under way at Mamaroneck in early 1926, but trains appear to be operating anyway. The New Haven's 1888 station, at left, was rolled back to accommodate. It still stood on this site in 2007. Harry F. Brown photo, author's collection.

Making the Best of Life

The NYW&B's gas-electric line car-crane helps string catenary for the Mamaroneck–Harrison extension in June 1927. Harry F. Brown photo, author's collection.

The joint New Haven–NYW&B station at Harrison, shown looking west from the NYW&B tracks about 1929. The station building dated to 1887 and, like all other NH stations on the joint line, was relocated to the west. Like Mamaroneck, it still stood in 2007. Harry F. Brown photo, author's collection.

This odd and rare 1928 view shows the NYW&B's first terminal at Rye while construction to this point was still under way. The camera looks east, which should raise knowledgeable eyebrows. Why? The NYW&B line is on the east side of the New Haven mainline instead of where it belongs on the west side. It is there temporarily while the NH station (at far left) is in the process of being relocated to make room for the permanent NYW&B line. Harry F. Brown photo, author's collection.

of 95 electric cars—more than one for every track mile—with a total seating capacity of 7,600 passengers.[8] Although owned by New Haven (and inconspicuously lettered "NYNH&HRRCO" next to their end doors), these last 50 cars were built to Westchester specifications and for its exclusive use. Thus despite a 15-year span between the Westchester's first and last cars, the entire fleet was nearly identical in looks and mechanical-electrical specifications; even so, they were still more advanced than comparable New Haven and New York Central equipment.

The White Plains Branch saw some improvements, too. While most of the route was still scantily populated, the section of White Plains served by the Westchester had grown steadily, and on November 7, 1926, the company opened a new station at the southeast end of the city to serve a housing development that had materialized from a onetime woodland. Located at Ridgeway, it had been planned from the beginning but postponed when the original builders decided that placing a station at Gedney Way to its north had better initial potential, with the planned Gedney Farm Hotel nearby. Ridgeway, of course, followed the new economy regime, with twin wood platforms and

Port Chester at last. The NYW&B had its own solid but modest terminal station just west of the New Haven's, which can be partly seen at the left. Jeffrey K. Winslow photo, October 1937, author's collection.

Just west of the Port Chester station, a westbound NYW&B train passes a Stamford-bound New Haven local. The unprepossessing NYW&B tower controlled the terminal crossovers and access to a storage yard behind the camera. Alfred Seibel photo, author's collection.

a small brick station building at the road underpass.[9] During the following summer, 13 express trains between White Plains and the Harlem River were added to the rush hour timetables. Unfortunately, though, the Westchester could never hope to be fully competitive with the New York Central between downtown White Plains and New York City; much of the branch's traffic had to come from outside the city's center and from the territory south of there.

Development in those areas was also steady, but slow and embarrassingly modest—quite unlike the Westchester's Port Chester line. The communities along the Sound shore from New Rochelle to Port Chester were a ready-made market. They had existed from colonial days and had steadily matured, nurtured first by the Boston Post Road and then, beginning in the late 1840s, by the New Haven. But its White Plains Branch territory was precisely the opposite and had to be developed from scratch by a railroad that, modern and efficient as it was, was working at a disadvantage.

Heathcote, or East Scarsdale, as it was originally called, was an all-too-typical example. Located about two miles east of Scarsdale's rapidly growing center (which was built around the New York Central station), Heathcote was the NYW&B's own creation. Its attractiveness as a suburb of its own depended entirely on the Westchester's attractiveness as a commuter carrier. Otherwise, it was simply a barely populated rural crossroads at Scarsdale's back door, with nothing there to create and support a self-sustaining community.

Since there was plenty of undeveloped land when the Westchester was built through the area, the railroad picked up acreage for residential and commercial development, as well as property alongside a short spur for potential freight customers. But it was not until the early 1920s that much was done with any of the land. In 1922, it resold 33 acres of intended residential property to the Heathcote Land Corporation for subdivision and further development, but eight years later, less than 30 percent of it actually had been built on. Other developers had about the same experience. The railroad also reserved some commercial property immediately around the station, and in 1923 an entrepreneur took the first plunge and built the Donnybrook Lodge, a striking English Tudor building designed by the notable New York architect Arthur L. Harmon. The Donnybrook housed a restaurant, five spacious upper-floor apartments, and three small stores (whose space became a bar at the end of Prohibition), and it typified the type of solid "Period" architecture that was becoming popular in Scarsdale and other southern Westchester County suburbs.[10] (Local lore states that in the early days, the Donnybrook's upstairs apartments served as a high-toned house of ill repute.) It was not until 1931 that a smaller and less pretentious version of the same style, housing some stores, was completed across the street. This, the Donnybrook Lodge, and an appropriately Tudor gasoline station constituted Heathcote's "business section" through the Depression. To do most of their shopping, residents drove over to the "real" Scarsdale or rode the NYW&B up to White Plains and took the Westchester Avenue trolley into the center of town.

Heathcote was also a more positive example of the Westchester's efforts to boost its freight service, still a stepchild but one that could grow with the county's building boom. In 1923 it sold some of its land immediately west of the Heathcote station to the Scarsdale Supply Company, which relocated its office and materials yard there from the New York Central line in downtown Scarsdale. The company remained a good customer for the rest of the railroad's life.

Looking just as lonely in the early 1960s as it did when built in 1923, the onetime Donnybrook Lodge stood across the street from the NYW&B's Heathcote station on property sold to its owner by the railroad. For ten years it was Heathcote's only commercial building, housing a restaurant and small stores. Scarsdale Public Library collection.

Hoping for more of the same, the astute and aggressive Leverett Miller in 1930 concluded that the railroad's freight future might be best tied to distribution warehouses in White Plains. By this time the city's retail district had become the shopping magnet for the central part of the county, and New York department stores were beginning to establish branches there. In May 1930, he proposed a warehouse center at the Westchester's relatively spacious but underused White Plains yard. Immediately afterward, he announced plans for an industrial park and Macy's warehouse at the Ridgeway station in the far southeast corner of the city, where there was a large amount of vacant land just west of the rail line.[11] But by then the Depression had begun, New Haven management thinking had changed, and no more was heard of anything.

As the Port Chester extension slowly moved eastward, the Westchester's traffic patterns swung east with it. The new line tapped the New Haven's heaviest commuting territory, and gradually became by far its principal traffic source. Now, impressive trains of up to eight cars could be seen whining along this line during the rush hours, the longest ever regularly run. Despite being shoulder-to-shoulder with the New Haven's Grand Central mainline, the Westchester's more frequent service, lower fares, and additional local stops succeeded in bringing in business, just as the New Haven had claimed it was meant to do. (But off-peak times were the same sad story, with minimal-size trains handling all the runs, generally two cars for the Port Chester Branch and one for White Plains. For much of the day, the semibucolic White Plains

Branch looked like a vastly overbuilt interurban line with its single cars clicking by every 20 minutes each way.)

The railroad always handled a substantial amount of intracity business within the Bronx, since from 180th Street north it passed through a developing area that had no subway or elevated service. From the railroad's inception at least into the late 1920s, about 20 percent of the Westchester's total passenger count (but certainly not its revenues) came from Bronx local riders. Said another way, the railroad really served as an extension of the subway through the northern Bronx, and in its earlier years its franchise required it to charge the subway's 5 cent fare for such riders. (In the 1920s, the company was allowed to raise its rate to 7 cents, and then to 10 cents in 1936.) Traffic between stations within Westchester County was also reasonably significant, amounting to 13.5 percent of total ridership in 1928.[12]

In the mid-1920s, the railroad also became a pioneer in coordinated bus-rail services by branching out into the feeder bus business. The genesis of the idea went back to the early 1900s, when the New Haven was buying up trolley companies in its territory to control competition. At the same time, though, it recognized their value as adjuncts to its passenger services and, in some cases, even as substitutes for financially hopeless local steam trains. In the process, it picked up two Westchester County trolley systems. First was the New York & Stamford Railway, which it put together in 1901 from two local lines that together linked New Rochelle and Stamford, Connecticut, paralleling the New Haven mainline through Larchmont, Mamaroneck, Harrison, Rye, and Port Chester. Then, presumably for the Westchester's benefit as feeder lines, the New Haven took control of a system radiating from White Plains in 1909. Rechristened the Westchester Street Railroad, it ran local streetcars in White Plains as well as long, rural routes reaching Scarsdale (with through service to Mount Vernon), Tarrytown, and Mamaroneck (including a short-lived Larchmont branch). Sometime after the Westchester got into business, the New Haven put both the New York & Stamford and Westchester Street Railroad under its management for day-to-day operations, apparently deciding that the Westchester was better situated to watch over the parent's New York State suburban satellites.[13]

But by 1925, the two railroads recognized both the shortcomings of the streetcar and the promise of the motor bus as a cheap, flexible supplement for their trains. Buses could reach places their trains did not go, help develop their suburban hinterlands, bring more passengers to their stations, and replace the obsolescent trolleys, which were proving financial losers anyway. Reportedly, the idea of a feeder bus network was the brainchild of Westchester president Leverett Miller—or at least he took credit for pushing it through. Probably not coincidentally, though, in the same year the New Haven formed its own intercity bus company, the New England Transportation Company, to operate longer routes in its territory. Its streetcar subsidiaries elsewhere in New England, such as the vast Connecticut Company, also were beginning to add buses to their rosters.

Two subsidiary bus companies emerged. First came the County Transportation Company, incorporated August 15, 1925, as a New York & Stamford Railway subsidiary, but funded with $250,000 of the New Haven's money and directly managed by the Westchester, a truly cooperative effort. County Transportation proceeded to map an ambitious system of 11 routes in Port Chester, Rye, Mamaroneck, Harrison, Larchmont, White Plains, and Scarsdale. Most were designed to feed joint New Haven–Westchester stations between New Rochelle and Port Chester, but early plans also included some lines built around NYW&B stations in White Plains and at Heathcote. One, for example, was a 3.4-mile line that wandered from the New York Central's Scarsdale station through the south part of the village and the north corner of New Rochelle before ending at the Westchester's Heathcote station. It took almost two years to get County into business, since it first had to obtain franchises (which another company also bid on), order equipment, and otherwise prepare for operation. In the process, some of these routes were dropped (including the meandering Scarsdale line, apparently), but in April 1926, the various individual shore municipalities awarded it 10-year franchises for eight lines.

County Transportation buses first hit the streets on April 3, 1927, and a pleased Miller promptly announced that "the company's buses have been exceptionally well received and well patronized." The system grew quickly; in 1929, it owned 60 buses, and by 1931 it was operating 13 routes along the shore line based at the reconverted New York & Stamford carbarn at Port Chester.[14]

By the time County Transportation went into business, the New Haven had put both the New York & Stamford and Westchester Street Railroad into receivership, with Westchester president Miller acting as receiver. In 1926 it decided to give up on the White Plains trolley network and sell it back to New York's Third Avenue Railway, which had owned it before 1909. Third Avenue, in turn, wasted little time substituting its own buses under its new Westchester Street Transportation name.[15]

Along with County Transportation's own new franchises, leases were arranged for New York & Stamford franchises and facilities, allowing the New Haven and Westchester to kill off NY&S trolley operations and substitute County buses. The Port Chester local streetcar lines became the first victims, ending April 3, 1927, and the New Rochelle–Stamford "main line" was converted between June and August. In late May or June, buses took over the NY&S branches to Rye Beach and Larchmont Manor. The New York & Stamford continued to exist as a shell corporation into the 1940s, primarily as County Transportation's owner and as the holder of some of County's franchises.[16]

To feed stations on its White Plains Branch, the Westchester acquired the Soundview Transportation Company in 1928 as its own wholly owned bus subsidiary. Soundview was a small, independently owned White Plains enterprise that had been incorporated May 11, 1921, and received its franchises early the next year. Its handful of routes changed frequently, but originally radiated from the New York Central's White Plains station and had only a nominal relationship to NYW&B territory. After the Westchester bought the company, four routes were established using eight buses, among which was a line to reach the Westchester's Gedney Way station in White Plains and another from White Plains to Heathcote.[17]

(Miller also planned a White Plains–Brewster bus route, perhaps to substitute for the stillborn Westchester Northern, but this never materialized. Possibly this was another reason he picked up Soundview, since it had White Plains franchises.)

The routes and schedules of County Transportation and Soundview were coordinated with the two railroads' train schedules, and this early form of intermodal passenger service did much to stimulate the development of the shore communities.[18] An extra boon came in 1928—coincidentally the same year that Westchester trains began running to Rye—when Playland, a large, beautifully planned family amusement park opened at Rye Beach. Afterward, the Westchester-County Transportation partnership never lacked for summer traffic. The precursor of today's theme parks (and now a National Historic Landmark), Playland instantly became the area's most popular summer attraction, with

County Transportation's Rye Beach route and charter trips disgorging hordes of families, couples, and loose teenagers at its commodious bus terminal.

Both companies proved reasonably profitable to their owners, too, even producing modest black figures during the worst of the Depression. Ultimately under direct New Haven control, County Transportation operated under its original name until 1957, when the railroad finally sold the interstate Stamford route to another company and the rest to the employees.[19] Following the Westchester's demise, the little Soundview company also ended up in the New Haven's bag of subsidiaries, but in 1950 it went back to independent ownership as the White Plains Bus Company.[20]

Somewhere in the mid-1920s, too, Miller coined "Metro-Urban" as the Westchester's official marketing name, attempting to distinguish his company's unique semi-rapid transit nature and feeder bus network from its more conventional railroad neighbors—and possibly also trying to give it a sophisticated Parisian air. Although he regularly used it in customer newsletters, speeches, and publicity, it never stuck with either the public or press, who habitually referred to the railroad as the "Westchester & Boston" or, perversely, the "Boston & Westchester."

The ever-vexing problem of the Westchester's New York City terminals also got considerable attention, albeit never a resolution. By 1925, the post–World War I suburban boom was accelerating dramatically, and the New York Central and New Haven began experiencing severe congestion at Grand Central, which had to cope with all suburban trains of both railroads, all of the Central's intercity traffic, and most of the New Haven's. The Westchester, on the other hand, was underutilized, despite its lower fares and generally superior service. Almost all its commuters were heading for points below 59th Street in Manhattan; by transferring at 180th Street or Hunt's Point, they had to endure long rides on crowded subway trains (often standing the entire trip), and therefore preferred to ride the New York Central or New Haven, even if it meant a drive to do so.[21] So began a succession of studies aimed at finding some way to channel all or most of everyone's suburban trains to some new corridor into the city that would distribute the loads better and take the pressure off Grand Central.

The New York City Transit Commission was the first to try with an admittedly partial solution. In 1925 Transit Commissioner Harkness offered a proposal to reroute all New Haven and Westchester suburban trains over the Hell Gate Bridge to a massive new terminal at Sunnyside in Queens, which also would be shared with the Long Island Rail Road. There passengers would transfer to either the IRT's Queensborough subway line to Grand Central (and soon to Times Square) or the Brooklyn–Manhattan Transit's line to 57th Street and Seventh Avenue, which continued down Seventh Avenue and Broadway.[22] The New Haven and Westchester rejected the idea on the rather reasonable grounds that its roundabout routing would lose time rather than save it, and the end result would be just another subway transfer, although much closer to downtown New York than the Bronx.

The Westchester's Leverett Miller then weighed in with his own plan in 1926. The Westchester—with private financing, he claimed—would build its own double-track tunnel and subway under the Harlem River, then run crosstown under 125th Street, ending at or near the Fort Lee ferry. En route, it would pass all the city's north-south subway and elevated lines, which would permit transfers within Manhattan and at least would avoid the long trips down from the Bronx. (A similar plan was proposed in 1929 by an engineering firm hired by the Harlem Board of Commerce, which doubtless was inspired by the business that such a subway might bring to the 125th Street area.)[23] But

A single car from White Plains approaches the Harlem River terminal in this 1937 view looking east. Jeffrey K. Winslow photo, author's collection.

this time the newly created Westchester County Transit Commission objected, citing the extra load it would put on the city rapid transit lines at that point and its disagreement with Miller's private financing method.

On March 1, 1926, almost immediately following the announcement of the so-called Miller Plan, the Westchester County Transit Commission issued the last of four reports. Put together by the engineering consulting firm of Parsons, Knapp, Brinckerhoff & Douglas, it proposed that the Westchester would be tied to the existing New York Central–New Haven line near 165th Street in the Bronx. From there, suburban trains of all three railroads would follow the Central's Harlem Division to Mott Haven at 149th Street, where they would be routed into a deep subway that crossed the river and ran below Madison Avenue and other streets to City Hall. Such a route would distribute suburban traffic over the Manhattan's entire length, touching all the major commercial and retail centers and ending within blocks of the Wall Street district.[24] Inevitably, however, the proposal bogged down over questions of financing, franchises, and cooperation among the three railroads. In the meantime, the Grand Central congestion problem was relieved when the New York Central installed a bidirectional signal system on its four-track mainline leading into the terminal, removing some of the need for a separate railroad subway.

Various other plans came and went, some of them proposing that the Westchester be tied directly to one of the subway lines—clearly impossible without substantial investment in new subway-compatible equipment and reelectrification to the subway's 600-volt DC third-rail system. Others contemplated a rail connection to the New Haven mainline at Columbus Avenue in Mount Vernon, allowing operation into Grand Central. (As noted in chapter 6, some minimal work was started on such a connection, although this was probably intended for New Haven Berkshire Division traffic moving via the Westchester Northern from Danbury rather than Westchester trains. In any event, the Westchester's cars were electrically unsuitable for operation over the New York Central's 600-volt DC third-rail system.) Such plans and arguments continued until the Depression finally put an end to all such talk, and the Westchester remained what it was and where it was.

But despite its lack of Manhattan terminals, the Westchester's business continued to grow dramatically, especially as the Port Chester extension worked its way eastward. In its startup year, ending June 30, 1913, the road carried slightly less than 2.9 million passengers and brought in $289,027 in revenue. Ten years later, the figure was 8.6 million, with operating revenues of $1.45 million; by 1928, the Westchester carried 14 million passengers and brought in $2.9 million in revenues, which more than qualified it for Class I railroad status. Much of this, of course, was attributable to Westchester County's burgeoning development, but nonetheless the NYW&B outperformed the New York Central and New Haven in its rate of traffic growth. For example, between 1914 and 1924 the Central's suburban traffic increased 134 percent, the New Haven's 138 percent, and the Westchester's 142 percent.[25] And overall, Westchester County was enjoying spectacular growth. Between 1920 and 1930, its population increased 51.2 percent, the largest in its history, most of it concentrated in the county's southern part.[26]

In short, all events seemed to point to eventual fulfillment of Morgan's dreams. His expectations for Westchester County had proven right, and his railroad no longer was an unnecessary piece of jewelry. It was now an essential part of the life of its communities, and its patrons felt it was there to serve them forever.

But they might have watched its financial performance and paused to think. Despite the constantly rising traffic volume and ever-improving operating ratio, deficits relentlessly worsened. The first-year loss of $1.4 million was fully expected of a brand-new operation, but instead of dropping as business improved, it only rose in succeeding years. During the early and mid-1920s, it averaged a bit less than $1.7 million, but by 1928 it had hit $1.9 million, and in 1929 it was just a hair short of $2 million. Why? In the boom year of 1929, the Westchester booked $2.5 million in revenues and only $1.6 million in direct operating expenses, giving it an operating profit of slightly over $960,000. Taxes of $276,000 reduced that to $684,000—still in the black. But then came what was labeled as "deductions from gross income" totaling almost $2.7 million. That represented unpaid bond interest (which the New Haven paid and held as a debt), other unreimbursed cash advances from the New Haven, and rentals. Based strictly on its operations, the Westchester was an efficient, profitable performer, but it could never catch up on its debts, which kept snowballing on its balance sheets.[27]

With both the national and local economies moving constantly upward, a solution possibly was in sight. By the late 1920s, the New Haven was experiencing its first flush of relative prosperity since the 1913 debacle, and if its situation continued to improve—which it showed all signs of doing—the parent might have simply forgiven its errant child, wiped out its accumulated indebtedness (which was so large that it could never be repaid anyway), and let it start over. After all, in 1929 the Westchester was able to cover 60 percent of its fixed charges for that year, so there was hope that it could be self-sufficient on a year-to-year basis if past debts were forgotten. In fact, had 1929's growth rate continued, this might well have happened within three or four years. But possible or not, any such speculation quickly became academic.

Troubles or no, the Westchester kept up its punctual operations. Heading for the Harlem River terminal, a Port Chester express crosses the Bronx River on the New Haven's Harlem River Branch. The movable bridge was one of the few occasional impediments to on-time performance. George Votava photo, November 1937, Dave Keller archive.

8

DOWN AND OUT (I): DOWN, 1930–1936

At this point, the author needs to relate a personal story. Shortly after I was born in 1931, my parents decided that Manhattan was not a place to raise a child, and so they looked for a house near relatives in Scarsdale. They found one at a bargain, but the reason for the bargain was not so cheery. Its owner, an architect specializing in upper-class suburban homes, had committed suicide in the house because his practice had vanished, leaving him with debts and no income.

An extreme example, to be sure, but it is sadly symbolic of what happened in Westchester County and everywhere else during those devastating years after 1929. In the business world, the Depression's two most vulnerable victims were railroads and real estate, particularly upper-class real estate. The suburban boom stopped dead; homes were sold and people moved to places where living costs and transportation were cheaper.

Another problem for the Westchester appeared, too. The suburbs naturally were a hotbed of automobile ownership, and the county was a pioneer in developing limited-access parkways. These were aesthetically designed in a park setting and limited to auto traffic, making them pleasurable to drive on and a welcome change from the congested county roads. Its first, the Bronx River Parkway, opened between the Bronx and Kensico Dam Park, north of White Plains, in 1925, paralleling the New York Central's Harlem Division its entire length. Following that came the Hutchinson River Parkway, which was completed between Pelham Manor and the outskirts of White Plains on October 31, 1928.[1] The Hutchinson River Parkway was built for higher speeds than its Bronx River predecessor, and it more directly affected the NYW&B. Its route began at the Boston Post Road (U.S. Route 1) in Pelham Manor and ran northeast roughly midway between the Westchester's White Plains Branch and the Port Chester line, ending at Westchester Avenue, only three miles east of the White Plains business center. Along the way, it almost adjoined the railroad through Mount Vernon, North Pelham, and Wykagyl, and came within a mile of Heathcote. It also lay within two or three miles of the Port Chester line and attracted traffic from that area, too. Ending as it did, just shy of the New York City limit, the new parkway was not designed as a high-speed access to Manhattan, and thus it had little effect on the Westchester's commuter business. But it did effectively drain away Westchester County local riders and served to accentuate the unfavorable economic balance between rush hour and midday traffic loads.

Beset by the twin blows of depression and increasing auto use, the Westchester lost a million riders a year between 1930 and 1931; by 1933 its operating income was 33 percent below the 1929 figure, while its deficit—a hair less than $2 million in 1929—was now $2.8 million.[2]

The New Haven was even worse off. By 1934 its operating revenues were less than half what they were in 1927, while it was still carrying all its debt burdens from the Morgan and Mellen era, including the Westchester.[3] Its trolley companies, bought so dearly in the early 1900s, were also now grievously suffering from both depression and the devastating effects of the private automobile, and they were forced to abandon lines and substitute buses where justified; most of the steamship lines were still doggedly kept operating, but they were living beyond their time. The New Haven's heavy but mostly unprofitable commuter business hardly helped, either.

Barely had the New Haven's and Westchester's fortunes reversed than the parent acted. On July 1, 1930, Leverett Miller, the Westchester's longtime president, retired at age 67—probably by request—and died only nine months later.[4] He was not replaced; instead, the New Haven took direct management control, clearing out all key officers from the handsome general office at 481 Morris Avenue and transferring their duties either to the New Haven's own headquarters or to local New Haven traffic agents in New York. New Haven president John J. Pelley became the Westchester's titular head—and a hostile one. Pelley was a newcomer to the New Haven, having arrived in the presidency a year earlier after a career in the Midwest and South with the Illinois Central and its Central of Georgia subsidiary. He brought with him an operating executive's cost-control discipline and, as an outsider, no ties to the New Haven's past. To Pelley, the Westchester was just another of the many mistakes of the past and now millstones of the present.

Changes came quickly. On July 28, 1930, basic daytime train service was cut in half, from its always-standard 20-minute headways to 40 minutes. Many rush hour trips were also pruned away. To nobody's surprise, patrons, community organizations, and municipalities loudly protested, and a compromise 30-minute service was agreed upon in August.[5] But the message was clear. Henceforth, the New Haven would do whatever it could to cut its losses from its wayward offspring. At the same time, the Westchester's communities realized that their railroad might have a shorter life than they supposed and that they needed to fight to keep it alive.

The crisis was not long in coming. The New Haven struggled to stay solvent during the early 1930s, cutting maintenance and borrowing money (including $16 million from the new federal Reconstruction Finance Corporation) to pay interest on its debt, but it was no use. On October 23, 1935, it petitioned the federal court in New Haven for reorganization under the recently enacted Section 77-B of the Federal Bankruptcy Act, and it formally entered bankruptcy on November 1.[6] Bankruptcy meant that the New Haven ceased paying interest on its own debt, which inevitably also included payments on its Westchester bond guarantee. Effectively disinherited, the Westchester had no choice but to follow, and on November 30 it joined its parent in reorganization.

The situation was hardly promising. *Time* magazine later summarized it: "Of 32 Class I U.S. railroads now undergoing reorganization [in 1937], none is more disorganized than the New York, New Haven and Hartford . . . and . . . of all the New Haven's tremendous grab-bag of securities, none is in a more pitiable state

A Port Chester express hurdles the Columbus Avenue viaduct in Mount Vernon. Alfred Seibel photo, 1937, author's collection.

A pastoral scene in the Hutchinson River valley on the New Rochelle–Port Chester Branch. Alfred Seibel photo, author's collection.

New Haven electrical engineer Harry F. Brown snapped this view of an NYW&B Port Chester train from the rear of his own eastbound New Haven local. Jack W. Swanberg collection.

than the New York, Westchester and Boston Railway Company."[7] In the 22 years preceding its bankruptcy, the New Haven had advanced the Westchester a total of $21.5 million, and it now realistically wrote the debt down to $1.[8]

The New Haven bankruptcy case, with the Westchester tagging along, were handed to Judge Carroll C. Hincks of the U.S. District Court in New Haven. Hincks then named Clinton L. Bardo to serve as the Westchester's trustee. Bardo, 68, was called out of retirement after a distinguished career in railroading and business management. Beginning as a telegrapher on the Pennsylvania Railroad, he served as a trainmaster on the Lehigh Valley, assistant superintendent on the New Haven, superintendent on the New York Central, and finally general manager on the New Haven. He moved on to become president of the New York Shipbuilding Company (and simultaneously vice president of American Brown-Boveri Electric Corporation). Entering his late 60s, he acted as head of the National Association of Manufacturers in 1934 and 1935, taking an important part in the controversies surrounding President Roosevelt's NRA codes.[9]

Bardo was given a stiff assignment on a short deadline. He was charged with operating the company, trying to make it self-supporting, and putting together a reorganization plan—if that were possible.[10] In doing so, he faced a multitude of intractable problems. Municipalities along the line demanded that their tax payments

Rolling south on the four-track Bronx speedway, a two-car Port Chester train has just passed the Baychester Avenue station. George Votava photo, May 1937, Dave Keller archive.

The White Plains terminal in its waning days. Bloomingdale Road is at the right; at left is the traveling overhead crane in the NYW&B's freight yard. Wm. Lichtenstern photo, Dave Keller archive.

A southbound train pauses at the joint NYW&B–NH station in Larchmont. Alfred Seibel photo, 1937, author's collection.

be kept up; they, too, were suffering from depression-depleted revenues, and in total the Westchester was paying them $300,000 a year. The New Haven, in desperate need of cash itself, wanted the money the Westchester owed it for electric power, track and property use, and rental of the 50 cars it had bought for the line during the 1920s. The three newly appointed New Haven trustees urged that the Westchester be liquidated and scrapped quickly to protect their company and security owners from further Westchester-connected outlays, which to them clearly would be money sucked into a black hole. Then there were the Westchester's bondholders, who now were receiving no interest and began pushing to protect their investments. Not helping matters, the City of New York ordered the company to rebuild two bridges in the Bronx to help ease problems caused by increased motor vehicle traffic, something the Westchester could not afford.[11] And finally, of course, Bardo had to deal with the steadily diminishing revenues while still maintaining a service level and quality that would keep from losing more riders. Getting all of that into some sort of orderly reorganization plan was to be done by August 3, 1936, less than nine months away.

The following two years were fully as tangled as those before the Westchester's construction, although far more public and less productive.

A five-car afternoon rush hour train speeds along the joint Port Chester right-of-way in 1928. Harry F. Brown photo, author's collection.

In May 1936, Bardo submitted his tentative plan to the court: he would apply for rate increases, attempt to have property taxes waived or reduced, negotiate with the various employee unions for wage cuts, and persuade the New Haven to declare a moratorium on rental payments. New Haven trustee Winthrop Daniels immediately objected on the basis that even if his railroad allowed the Westchester to use the New Haven's power, track, and equipment free, its suddenly destitute subsidiary still would be unable to cover its other expenses. Daniels then urged to court to stop Bardo from operating the company and allow its liquidation.[12]

A modicum of relief came from the New York Transit Commission on July 22, 1936, when it allowed the Westchester to raise its intracity fares from 7 cents to 10 cents.[13] It was a help, but not much.

Otherwise, though, Bardo got cooperation from almost nobody. Taxes were a sore point, especially when it became clear that the company's 1936 revenues would not be enough to cover them after deducting operating expenses. On June 5, Bardo notified White Plains that the Westchester could not pay its $19,235 city tax, which had just fallen due, adding that this and other taxes could never be paid unless "the patrons who use the railroad, and the officers and employees who operate it, and the communities served by it, are willing to step into the breach and make some reasonable sacrifices."[14] He

It is a quiet afternoon (unfortunately, there were many) at the Westchester Avenue terminal in White Plains as a local prepares to load for the Harlem River. George Votava photo, December 1937, Bob's Photo collection.

made the rounds of all the municipalities that taxed the railroad, begging for some form of relief; with singular shortsightedness, each rejected his proposals, reasoning that the Westchester never really would be abandoned, and thus tax reductions were unnecessary and harmful to them.[15]

In the hope of lowering manpower costs—always the largest operating expense—Bardo petitioned the Interstate Commerce Commission to have the company exempted from the jurisdiction of the Railway Labor Act and asked the employees to take a 10 percent wage cut. Everyone refused. The ICC ruled that although the Westchester was an intrastate carrier itself, it was "still an integral part of the New Haven system," and so was bound by the interstate commerce laws.[16] That one must have especially rankled, since the New Haven obviously wanted no part of the railroad and, in fact, was publicly saying it should be scrapped immediately. At the same time, the labor unions replied that they could not accept a wage reduction. Like the various taxing authorities, they felt that the Westchester could not possibly cease operations and, in their case, the workers hoped for some form of public takeover.[17]

Finally, there was the rentals demon. Bardo persuaded Judge Hincks to allow him to hire the Coverdale & Colpitts engineering consulting firm to look into the entire array of New Haven–Westchester financial relationships, particularly the reasonableness of the various agreements for power usage, property rental, and trackage rights. Their conclusions were of no help either; essentially the consultants felt that the New Haven's seemingly high demands were justified because of the leased property's value. (In an uncharacteristic gesture of help, the New Haven had recently reduced the Harlem River–174th Street line rental from $109,000 to $12,000 a year, but the consultants felt that even the old amount was fair.) They, too, joined the chorus insisting that the only solution was dissolution.[18]

Unable to work out a successful plan, Bardo submitted his report to Judge Hincks as required in August. Hincks responded in a letter made public on September 2, acknowledging the trustee's expense reductions and his failure to obtain tax or wage concessions. He then noted that, aside from wages and rentals, "there appear to me to be absolutely no other items on your operating statements that are susceptible of reduction, unless it be taxes." Continuing with an urgent appeal for cooperation, the judge said:

> Indeed there is scarcely time for [litigation of tax assessments]. For it looks doubtful, to put it mildly, whether we can keep the road running long enough to await the result of such litigation.
>
> Instead, it is my view that we should give all parties affected an opportunity and the resulting responsibility each to make his own equitable contribution to save the road. The court, with your [i.e., Bardo's] assistance, will, at least for a month or two longer, keep the wheels rolling and make arrangements so that at the end of that time we can say to the traveling public, to the municipalities served by the road, and to the employees:
>
> Here are the irreducible figures: Our gross revenues, even with the fares recently increased, are so much and we can count on no more. Our operating expenses are so much, and we can cut them no further unless labor will accept a voluntary wage reduction, or unless the taxing authorities will give effect to our lack of earnings by reducing tax assessments. . . .
>
> If no concessions are forthcoming, we may fairly conclude that the employees do not care enough about their jobs or the municipalities do not care enough about the transportation facilities furnished by the road to justify its further operation. It will thus be demonstrated that there is no economic justification for further continuance of the road.[19]

Thus, with the judge's permission, Bardo continued his day-to-day combat, hoping for a miracle. Using his railroad management expertise, he also did what he could to economize, while still maintaining service quality. For example, he installed remote door controls to cut down crew size on long trains, and introduced train-handling methods that would reduce electric power use. In the meantime, both the bondholders and riders took the situation seriously enough to organize and come up with their own solutions. From the start, the bondholders were split into two factions: one supporting the hope that under a reorganization plan the company could somehow be made profitable, the other wanting a quick liquidation to salvage what assets they could while praying that their bonds would be well treated in the New Haven's reorganization.

The larger group, formed in December 1936 and headed by Irving A. Sartorius, decided to try its own reorganization plan, which it promptly published. The Westchester, it proposed, would first be corporately divorced from the New Haven. Then, in effect, it would revert to what the original NYW&B and New York & Port Chester promoters had envisioned in the early 1900s, that is, an extended rapid transit line. The existing 11,000-volt AC electrification would be scrapped and its long, heavy cars sold. At the same time, it would be reelectrified using the subway and elevated lines' 600-volt DC third-rail system and reequipped with 50 lightweight subway-compatible cars that would operate directly into Manhattan on the city rapid transit lines. It seemed a logical plan that could be accomplished at a relatively low cost, but it also assumed that the Westchester's earnings would improve to the point where financing would be possible. And, being a bondholder plan, it insisted that there would be no waiver of the New Haven's bond guarantee.[20]

Those last two requirements doomed the Sartorius plan. In early 1936, the Interstate Commerce Commission ordered the railroads, including the New York Central and New Haven, to cut their regular passenger fares from 3.6 cents per mile to 2 cents.[21] Since one of the Westchester's chief advantages was its lower rates, it could only watch its passengers defect, particularly on the Port Chester line, which adjoined the New Haven its full length. In the first seven months of the year, it lost 368,000 passengers to the New Haven alone.[22] So instead of picking up, the unhappy railroad's traffic dropped 5 percent between 1935 and 1936, hitting an all-time low. The other provision, demanding "full performance of the [New Haven's] guaranty to the total amount, and unpaid interest," was not only blatantly self-serving but also absurdly unrealistic. Needless to say, the New Haven emphatically objected, but beyond that it looked clear to all other parties involved that the bondholders expected everyone except them to make sacrifices.

Although the Sartorius plan died, an interesting and long-forgotten relic came to light in the late 1980s, when a proposal drawing made by the Edward G. Budd Manufacturing Company dated September 4, 1936, was discovered in the carbuilder's old files. Budd had introduced the technique of shotwelding stainless steel, and in the early 1930s it proceeded to make itself a pioneer in lightweight, stainless steel streamlined railroad equipment. (It went on to become a major railroad carbuilder, lasting into the early 1980s and producing two generations of Amtrak equipment.) Always both creative and aggressive, Budd undoubtedly was following the Westchester's travails and the bondholders' planning; in response, it proposed an 81-foot-long two-section lightweight articulated car for the Westchester, seating 96 passengers, similar in concept and appearance to Budd's so-called Zephyr experimental five-unit articulated built for the Brooklyn–Manhattan Transit in 1934. (Other builders produced somewhat similar experimental lightweight five-unit articulated cars for the BMT between 1934 and 1936.) The car was designed for subway and elevated clearances, and it would have been light enough to operate on the elevated lines. Presumably it could have run directly into Manhattan either over the Third Avenue elevated from the Harlem River or on the IRT subway from 180th Street.[23]

The second group to add its voice was a committee composed of Westchester commuters and freight customers. Headed by William E. Schramek of Larchmont, the Citizens Committee for Continuance was more practical about the financial situation than the Sartorius group and urged operation by some sort of public body. The committee won the privilege of participating in all planning activities relating to the line, and it became increasingly influential as the proceedings went on.[24]

The Westchester ended 1936 with a $3 million deficit, only slightly improved from the year before, although either figure was largely academic, since it included all unpaid (and never to be paid) taxes, rentals, and bond interest.[25] The trains were still running on their old schedules, but a single car or, at most, a two-car train was more than sufficient for non-rush hour business. Damaged equipment was no longer repaired but instead was cannibalized to keep the fleet running.

The next step, unfortunately, was inevitable.

This five-car New Rochelle rush hour express exudes prosperity, but the Westchester had fewer than three days to live. George Votava photo, December 29, 1937, Dave Keller archive.

9

DOWN AND OUT (II): OUT, 1937–1942

It was unthinkable, but there it was. On April 3, 1937, Judge Carroll Hincks finally announced that the trusteeship had failed, and he ordered Clinton Bardo to show cause why the reorganization should not be ended. May 25 was the final date for filing claims against the trustee.[1] To protect themselves, the bondholders now pressed for dissolution, and the New Haven threatened repossession of its right-of-way and cars if some cash payments were not forthcoming. Short of some miracle, the Westchester would die.

Bardo's final report and the formal end of the trusteeship came June 28. In his report Bardo listed cash assets of $274,632 and liabilities of more than $51 million; the Westchester's book value had dropped $8 million since 1936, and its total accumulated deficit stood at $50.6 million. It needs to be noted again, though, that by this time the Westchester's balance sheet was largely an accounting fantasy that completely obscured its true financial state. Not only were the huge liability items meaningless, but attorney James L. Dohr, the Westchester's last receiver, found an $8 million item on the assets side labeled "intangible assets." When he asked what that represented, nobody knew. It later turned out that it represented part of that infamous $11 million spent in acquiring the old NYW&B and New York & Port Chester assets before 1909. It also should be mentioned that despite its clearly perilous financial state, the Westchester was still managing to cover its direct day-to-day operating expenses and did so through 1937. Despite a 13 percent revenue drop between 1936 and 1937, the operating ratio for that last dismal year came out at 82—not healthy but, considering the circumstances, not bad either.[2]

At the same session, the judge approved a bondholder suit to transfer the railroad to an equity receivership, which normally would lead to liquidation.[3] The Westchester case then left the federal court at New Haven and migrated to the U.S. District Court in New York City, where it was assigned to Judge John C. Knox.[4] Bardo was asked to remain as trustee until the receivers could be appointed to supervise the liquidation. Unhappily, he never made it to the end; he died of a stroke August 31 while on an inspection trip over the railroad.[5]

Upon Bardo's death, Judge Knox immediately appointed Dohr and former federal judge Edwin L. Garvin as receivers. Although they had little chance of keeping the Westchester running, they made some halfhearted tries. Dohr, particularly, felt that something still might be done to relieve the company's three major headaches: its taxes, New Haven rentals, and labor costs.

A typical lonely White Plains Branch run heads north near Gedney Way in White Plains. George Votava photo, May 1937, Dave Keller archive.

The receivers did not get off to an auspicious start. With singular lack of foresight, the employees picked this particular time to call a strike. Dohr and Garvin quickly commandeered a coach in the Morris Park yards, where they met with the union leaders and talked them out of any immediate action. But they got no agreement on wage reductions or work rule changes.

Rentals were another lost cause. Bardo's 1936 Coverdale & Colpitts study hardly helped the receivers' cause, but nonetheless Dohr became a regular commuter between New York and New Haven to try to negotiate with Howard Palmer, the principal New Haven trustee. In the end, though, Palmer best summarized his attitude by telling Dohr, "Hell, those people in Westchester have had free transportation long enough."[6]

The tax situation was no better, either. Although most Westchester communities had received little or no tax payments since 1935, they almost universally deemed it impossible to reduce the assessments. The sole exception was New Rochelle's mayor, Harry Scott, who offered to cut his city's taxes in half if the other communities did the same. But everyone else demurred, fearing a precedent that might be extended to other properties.[7]

For their part, the Westchester's bondholders now united to insist that any reorganization was impossible, and they joined the New Haven in pressing for abandonment. In mid-October, Judge Knox partially acquiesced to the New Haven's demand that the Westchester be dispossessed of all its property, and allowed service abandonment between New Rochelle and Port Chester. The Port Chester extension, of course, was on New Haven right-of-way, and its owner hoped eventually to salvage its track and wire for use elsewhere; unfortunately, it was also the Westchester's heaviest source of traffic. (The New Haven also wanted the Westchester off its Harlem River Branch, but the judge refused this as being crippling to whatever future the railroad had.) A short jurisdictional squabble ensued between Judge Knox and the New York State Public Service Commission, which had authority over rates and services, but the federal judge went ahead, state commission permission or no. The New Haven agreed to keep the track and wire intact for the time being, should some miracle occur to save the Westchester.[8]

Five minutes late, the last train for Port Chester cleared the Harlem River terminal platform at 11:35 p.m. on October 31, carrying newspaper reporters and mourning railroad enthusiasts among its 40-odd passengers. Five minutes later, the last train left Port Chester. The next day, 104 employees were laid off as the eastern mainline terminus was cut back to the North Avenue station in New Rochelle, where it had been before 1921, and the $5 million Port Chester extension was left to rust less than 10 years after its full completion.[9]

Belatedly awakening to the prospect of losing their railroad, the Westchester communities began mobilizing. The Citizens Committee for Continuance dramatically declared that the Westchester's abandonment would cause "incalculable damage to communities throughout Westchester County, virtually affecting every phase of economic life."[10] A hurried meeting of officials from all Westchester-served municipalities was called in White Plains on December 4 and resulted in a tentative offer to cut the 1936 and 1937 tax assessments in half. The officials also declared their support for the Citizens Committee's plan to create a state transit authority with power to acquire and operate the railroad.[11]

But by then it was too late. On December 18, Judge Knox reluctantly signed the death order after being told by the receivers and the bondholder representatives that the company was "hopelessly insolvent" and could never be profitable, even with the tax reductions. Saying, "I have no more right to extend the service than I have the right to give part of the road's cash to a mendicant on the streets," he set December 31, 1937, as the Westchester's last day.[12]

On New Year's Eve, a bottle of champagne was smashed over the front of a single electric car, wielded by a man who, as a three-year-old, had watched the first New York, Westchester & Boston train arrive at the bright new Westchester Avenue terminal in 1912—and was now bidding good-bye to the last. On such "last trip" occasions elsewhere, the person with this kind of experience was usually some grizzled old-timer who tottered in to do the honors. Not so here; this man was all of 28.

The one-car train itself, scheduled to leave at 11:41 p.m., was held up nine minutes as New Year's Eve celebrants crowded around it blowing its horns and their own noisemakers. At New Rochelle, the last train got off for New York at 11:57, two minutes late and barely beating the arrival of 1938. Final runs left the Harlem River for White Plains at 11:50, and the very last, for New Rochelle, at midnight. It arrived 26 minutes later at North Avenue with five people aboard, ending all Westchester service. No photos were taken, and no newspaper reporters were on hand for interviews. On New Year's Day, the Westchester was dead at age 25. Its 287 employees were out of work, and the *New York Times* estimated that some 18,000 riders were looking up New Haven and New York Central schedules. On Monday, January 3, the first regular workday after the holiday, the New Haven added 40 extra cars to its schedules and the New York Central added 16, but both railroads still suffered overcrowding.[13]

The wheels were no longer rolling, but the Westchester was not yet dead. In his order, Judge Knox had specified that all track, wire, cars, and stations were to be left intact

The Westchester's life was ebbing away as George Votava photographed this express on the NYW&B's dedicated track near the Harlem River terminal in November 1937. The fill was part of the approach to the New Haven's Hell Gate Bridge tracks. Dave Keller archive.

for an unspecified period while the various political bodies tried to come up with some alternative method of operation. A skeleton crew was kept on to patrol the line daily in a motor track car and watch over the stations and stored cars. The New Haven reclaimed the 50 cars it had bought and leased to the railroad. Since they were electrically unsuitable for use in the New Haven's own Grand Central service, it stripped them of their electrical gear, modified their carbodies, and put them in steam-hauled suburban service out of Boston. (In 1951, 20 of these got a third life when they were shipped to Saudi Arabia to carry oil field workers.) The remaining 45 cars, theoretically owned by the Westchester's creditors, were moved to storage at the Morris Park yards, awaiting either sale or a recall to service.[14] (Actually, only 42 cars could be called usable; 3 had been wreck-damaged in the final years and stripped for parts.)

Shortly afterward, and perhaps inevitably, the powerful (and automobile-minded) Robert Moses proposed an express highway to be built over the right-of-way between the Bronx and New Rochelle—an idea bitterly opposed by the communities along the line who feared loss in property valuations and property taxes should the railroad somehow be saved.[15] Instead, they finally began to make serious efforts to revive the railroad before it was too late. At one point in early 1938, the company's former employees even offered to work without pay, to be reimbursed retroactively once the railroad was back on its feet. Their plea perhaps looks either naïve or disingenuous, but the Depression had not yet ended (in fact, 1937 was a setback year), and many of them had not found new jobs.[16] Some did eventually go to work for the New Haven and New York Central, starting again at the bottom of the seniority ladder.

New York City had the most serious interest in using the railroad's right-of-way—or at least a part of it. The area of the Bronx served by the Westchester had been rela-

Now idle for three years, the Westchester's remaining car fleet lines up disconsolately at East 174th Street in the Bronx. The New Haven is at the right. Author's collection.

The New Haven–owned NYW&B cars went right on carrying commuters, but behind steam power out of Boston. Still displaying their arch windows but sans center doors, three such veterans climb the grade at Sharon, Massachusetts, en route to Providence. L. Walter photo, September 1946, Jack W. Swanberg collection.

tively undeveloped when the line opened, but several communities had now grown up around its stations. Without the railroad, they were left to rely solely on local bus and trolley routes, and any further development was inhibited as well. Political pressures began building to preserve and perhaps enhance the rapid transit service that this area depended on by integrating the idle four-track right-of-way into the city subway system. That idea would take time to jell, but it was the most immediately promising, since the Bronx section was all within one municipality and thus it could be accomplished without having to get agreements and financing from a lot of smaller communities. But this idea would only involve the New York City section, between the 180th Street station and the Bronx-Westchester boundary. Beyond there, many people had proposals, but for various reasons none were practical. In the end, nobody seemed to know what to do.

State Senator Pliny Williamson, a Scarsdale lawyer representing central Westchester County, introduced a bill in the legislature that would create a public railroad authority, composed of 18 commissioners, to take over all or part of the New York, Westchester & Boston and operate it.[17] By this time, public authorities operating transportation facilities were nothing new to New York; the concept had been pioneered by the Port Authority of New York in 1921 and dramatically expanded by the legendary hero/villain Robert Moses. Municipal ownership and unification of the city's entire rapid transit network was also then in the works and finally accomplished in 1940. But Williamson's Westchester authority was the first to involve a private suburban railroad serving two counties (ruled by different political parties) and a variety of municipalities—and that seemed to be the sticking point. Although the Williamson bill passed in March 1938, Governor Herbert Lehman vetoed it. Lehman maintained: "It is unwise to have government create a public benefit corporation with color of governmental authority and sanction for the purpose of acquiring and operating a private railroad running through several communities, which has been forced to discontinue operations." Such bodies, he said, should be created only for "very special purposes."

One of the bill's principal opponents was New York's mayor, Fiorello LaGuardia, who was then wrestling with the $300+ million projected cost of taking over the IRT and BMT systems. LaGuardia was happy enough to include the NYW&B's Bronx section in his soon-to-be-unified city rapid transit system, but in no mood to help subsidize Westchester County riders. He managed to find a major legal flaw in the bill's wording, which had appointed the Bronx borough president to act for the city in the state's takeover of the line—a violation, he claimed, of the city's home rule charter that gave such power to the Board of Estimate. The bill thus had to be rewritten or, in LaGuardia's opinion, forgotten entirely. Perhaps significantly, it was never resubmitted.[18]

Williamson continued to press, and he finally forced the governor to form a committee to study the problem and come up with a politically palatable solution. Appointed August 25, 1938, the group consisted of Williamson and such notables as New Deal brain-trusters Adolph A. Berle and Rexford G. Tugwell. (By then Berle was a veteran of this sort of thing, having recently helped put together a preliminary plan for full public ownership of New York City's rapid transit system.) The committee then embarked on a six-month study.

Concurrently, Irving Sartorius and his Westchester bondholders were back at work, and once again they reversed themselves. Having demanded full liquidation a year earlier, they now concluded that a scrap sale would net "practically nothing" and that they were ready for another try at reorganization. In April 1938, Sartorius announced a plan to cut expenses that involved the old standbys of tax relief, labor cost concessions, and reducing the New Haven rentals. To further achieve the economy goals, train service would be cut almost 50 percent from its old level, and five stations would be closed. But, of course, the bondholders remained adamant that one major expense was sacrosanct and untouchable: bond interest payments and the New Haven's guarantee were to be continued unaltered. (Stubbornly optimistic though the bondholders may have been, the bond market felt otherwise; Westchester bonds hit a low of 4 in 1938.)[19]

The year ended with nothing concrete accomplished. The railroad was now one of the living dead. It was still intact as far as New Rochelle and White Plains and, in theory, ready to run again whenever the call came. But a year's neglect had taken its toll; weeds now flourished as ties decayed and equipment and fixtures rusted. For all practical purposes, the New Rochelle–Port Chester section was irretrievably gone. The "Great Hurricane of 1938" smashed into the Connecticut shoreline on September 21, devastating large parts of the New Haven's mainline, among much else. New Haven crews wasted no time in pulling out the old Westchester rail, ties, and wire to help piece their railroad back together. At the same time, the New Haven sold or demolished the small way stations that had been built exclusively for Westchester use. The right-of-way was still there, and parts are still visible today, but it would need to be completely rebuilt for operation. (The Port Chester terminal and the little brick structure at Larchmont Gardens were lucky survivors; they still stood in 2007, well-maintained but shorn of platforms and stairways.)[20]

Governor Lehman's blue-ribbon committee finally made its report in February 1939. It recognized that private operation was financially hopeless and recommended public ownership—but not by some special new body. Instead, the group felt that the Port Authority of New York should acquire the Westchester and operate it. A bill incorporating this suggestion was drawn up, but it died in committee in Albany. That ended the idea of a public takeover of the entire system; Lehman dissolved the committee at the end of May, concluding, "I do not know what else can be done."[21] Unfortunately, the public-ownership advocates were pioneering what was then a radical concept for suburban railroad operations; they were fighting not only inertia but a political climate of fragmented jurisdictions, fears of large new expense commitments, and loss of tax revenues. And in trying to overcome all of this, they were also dealing from a position of weakness. Of all the major New York area suburban railroads, the Westchester was, to be blunt, the most expendable. (True, there were perennial waifs like the New York Central's Putnam Division, but these still had the protection of large companies that supposedly could afford to indulge them.) Although the Westchester's constituency was vocal, stubborn, and well-heeled, it was not large enough and, in truth, not seriously inconvenienced enough to overcome the basic political resistance and the various jurisdictional jealousies.

The remainder of 1939 slogged on with no other workable solutions in sight. Various last-ditch proposals came and went. A group of independent businessmen showed interest in buying the line if it could obtain tax relief, but that idea went nowhere. Regardless of who was proposing what, the municipalities were afraid to commit themselves to any waivers or reductions.[22]

The coffin was beginning to close, and in May 1939 the New Haven pushed down the lid by increasing its local train services in the Port Chester–New Rochelle–Mount

Vernon area to 30-minute daytime headways, the same as the Westchester had offered. That undercut one more justification for the line's revival.[23]

Taking the first step to end the agony, the court ordered the sale of all copper overhead wire on June 9; it also set October 8 as the date for final hearing on complete dismantlement.[24] Further conferences among Westchester County officials followed with no results, and on November 10 Judge Knox formally ordered the line's sale and demolition, to be effective January 5, 1940. New York City already had offered to buy the Bronx portion of the right-of-way—technically as a substitute for the uncompleted Concourse line of the Independent Subway, but in practice as an adjunct to the IRT's White Plains Road line. Left marooned, Westchester County still held out hope of inducing the Port Authority to take over the section north of the city, which it hoped could be tied into the city's planned operation. With those proposals pending, the judge, probably heaving a resigned sigh, agreed to postpone the receivers' request for dismantlement—first for a week, then until October 4. During that time, five of the railroad's principal Westchester County communities united to hire the engineering firm of B. J. Van Ingen & Company to study the possibilities of public financing and operation of the county portion for presentation to the Port Authority.[25]

In the meantime, Mayor LaGuardia reached an agreement with James Dohr, the receiver, to purchase the Bronx segment between the 174th Street–West Farms junction and the northern city limits near the Westchester's Dyre Avenue station. The sale was signed April 17, 1940, giving the Westchester bondholders $1.875 million for the 4.5 miles of four-track line, stations, and the 180th Street station-office building. The fate of the Westchester County lines remained unresolved, awaiting the Van Ingen engineering study and the Port Authority's decision.[26]

The city went ahead on the conversion work, which entailed removing the catenary from the two local tracks, installing third rails and other fixtures for 600-volt DC operation along with a new signal system, and modifying station platforms for the narrower IRT cars. Pending a decision on the Westchester County portion, the two center express tracks were left intact along with their overhead catenary, under the assumption that if the Port Authority proposal was successful, the agency would run its trains over them to 180th Street.

The patient Judge Knox granted several more demolition postponements, but in May 1941 the Port Authority announced it was not interested in operating the line. That was all. On May 23, Judge Knox directed the receiver to begin removing the tracks, bridges, catenary towers, and other steelwork—all of which the federal government already had prudently bought for its defense buildup. Under pressure from the government, Lipsett, Inc., the scrapping contractor, hustled to the job. Leased New Haven steam locomotives, hauling wrecking cranes and gondola cars, were dispatched to White Plains and New Rochelle and began working their depressing way south. (Helping, too, was the Westchester's own gas-electric line car-crane.) By 1942, 15,000 tons of steel had been recovered. Most of the rails were reused, and the bridges and catenary towers were cut up and melted down for munitions.[27]

(As a postscript to this sorry story, the Port Authority—ever-zealous to protect its credit rating, buoyed by the profits from its bridge and tunnels—repeated its Westchester behavior in the late 1950s when it refused to take over the bankrupt Hudson & Manhattan Railroad. It was finally forced to do so in 1962, creating the present PATH operation.)

All was not gone, though. At 11:11 a.m. on May 15, 1941, Mayor LaGuardia, decked out in a subway motorman's cap, snipped a red, white, and blue ribbon stretching across the stairway at the Westchester's old 180th Street station and thus inaugurated the first regular train service over the old Westchester in three and a half years.[28] Granted, it was only four miles long, but still very much the Westchester in physical appearance. Along with 180th Street, the original Westchester stations at Morris Park, Pelham Parkway, Gun Hill Road, Baychester Avenue, and (in part) Dyre Avenue were refurbished and re-opened. At the time, all four tracks were still also there, along with their catenary towers and wire over the two center express tracks, awaiting a Port Authority decision. (Somewhat oddly, although the resuscitated line was in effect an extension of the Interborough Rapid Transit subway and operated with IRT equipment, it was actually manned and managed by the city's Independent Subway division, with which it had no physical connection.)

But otherwise, the new operation was hardly up to its predecessor's standards. Once the Westchester County scrapping operations were finished, the catenary supports and two center express tracks were removed, leaving only some remnants used for car storage. (The New Haven connection at 174th Street was also left intact for several years.) In place of the Westchester's long, commodious steel cars were two-car sets of 1907 wooden open-platform IRT elevated cars recently dispossessed by the demolition of the Ninth Avenue elevated. Nor was the service itself any improvement. The "Dyre Avenue Shuttle" was just that—a shuttle between the Westchester's 180th Street station and Dyre Avenue. Passengers still disembarked at 180th Street and trudged through the old Westchester connecting corridor to the subway after a creaking ride that might work its way up to 35 mph. It was not until 1957 that a direct connection was built between the two lines and some Broadway–Seventh Avenue trains began running directly to Dyre Avenue—finally giving the Westchester, or what was left of it, the through service it should have had from the beginning.[29] As of 2007, Westchester aficionados could ride it as the north end of the No. 5–Lexington Avenue express service.

The Westchester's remaining cars, which had sat inertly at the Morris Park yard since the end of 1937, were moved out of the way when the city took over this section. First they were shoved south to sit on the West Farms viaduct below the 180th Street station. Then they were hauled to the New York Central's Port Morris yard in the Bronx. With the country at war in 1942, defense industries needed railroad equipment quickly, and the U.S. Maritime Commission snatched them up and dispatched them to Texas to carry workers for the Houston Shipbuilding Company plant. After the war's end, some went to carry oil workers in Santa Fe Springs, California, some went to the U.S. Army for service at Aberdeen Proving Ground in Maryland, a few were used for emergency housing in Salt Lake City, and three even wandered to the Cerro de Pasco tin mine in Peru. (Amazingly, at least one remained intact in Peru in 2007.) The Westchester's sole electric locomotive went to the New Haven to work alongside its identical sisters; after helping to dismantle the line, the unique gas-electric line car-crane was scrapped.[30]

The well-designed Westchester car shop building easily found a new industrial life. So, too, did many of the stations, which were handsome, solid, and in many cases originally designed to house stores or offices. With its graceful lines, soaring vaulted ceiling, generous expanses of glass, and large open floor space, the Quaker Ridge station quite naturally became an artist's home and studio, with flower pots gracing the platform. (It

Better than nothing. A southbound "Dyre Avenue shuttle" leaves the former NYW&B Baychester Avenue station in May 1947. The Westchester's Baychester tower is ahead of the train, out of service since the early 1930s, but still standing uselessly. George Votava photo, Dave Keller archive.

A pair of 1907 elevated cars waits for Dyre Avenue passengers at the regal East 180th Street NYW&B station and office building in 1951. Author's photo.

The White Plains terminal as it looked in 1947, before the site became a B. Altman department store. Author's photo.

remained a well-kept residence in 2007.) And along the "Dyre Avenue shuttle" line, the original stations remained to serve trains, humbler though they were. Happily, the grandest of all, the 180th Street station and general office building, was among those surviving into 2007 in its original form, owned and occupied by New York's Metropolitan Transportation Authority and listed on the National Register of Historic Places. Some buildings found no buyers, among them the handsome White Plains terminal, which underwent two ironic reincarnations. Originally located on the unfashionable back side of the city's commercial district, it sat vacant until 1950, when it was demolished, to be reborn as an expanded branch of New York's popular B. Altman's department store chain. In 1995, the now-obsolescent Altman's disappeared, and in its place appeared a Nordstrom Branch in "The Westchester," an emphatically upscale shopping mall. Other orphans were simply left to decompose for a decade or so more. A few of these unfortunates, now reduced to forlorn, gaping, and sometimes dangerous concrete shells, still stood in 2007.

The Westchester's life finally whimpered to an end on May 10, 1946, when James Dohr made the last payout on assets sold. On June 28, the court discharged him, his job finished.[31]

Looking north at Columbus Avenue Junction before and after. The "before" view was shot in 1937 from a Port Chester train crossing the White Plains Branch. In the background is the East Lincoln Avenue, Mount Vernon station. "After" dates to 1947. Since then, the tower has been demolished and nothing remains of the old scene. "Before" by Alfred Seibel, author's collection; "after," author's photo.

The rear of Heathcote station as it looked in 1951, now given over to nature. The tower in the left rear is the former Donnybrook Lodge. Author's photo.

The NYW&B in 1997, some distance from Westchester County. Stored at Lima, Peru, ENAFER No. 203 had been passed down from the U.S. Maritime Commission to Peru's Cerro de Pasco mining operation. Jack W. Swanberg photo, author's collection.

That left only some saddened, frustrated historians and railroad enthusiasts to ponder and argue all the "what ifs?" that might have rescued the railroad: What if one of the proposed 1920s era downtown tunnels had actually been built? What if the taxing authorities, labor unions, and New Haven had been more farsighted and flexible during the late 1930s? What if Westchester trains could have been rerouted to Grand Central or Penn Station? What if the line's surrealistic balance sheet had been wiped clean and restructured on a more pragmatic operating basis? What if the line had been reequipped for through operation over the city subway system—or built that way originally? What if public ownership had been achieved?

Today it takes some looking to find relics of the "super railroad" among the apartment houses, shopping centers, and stores of its old Westchester County territory. Some stations still exist, ranging in condition from beautifully kept, to occupied but altered, to outright ruins. Part of the right-of-way in southeast White Plains is a walking path, and some short pieces of highway occupy the line in Heathcote and New Rochelle. Otherwise, the hard-core Westchester archaeologist can find a depressing array of concrete bridges and culverts, tree-shrouded fills, vegetation-filled gashes through hills, highway bridges over nothing, and vacant bridge abutments.

And in the meantime, much has happened since the Westchester died. Its territory was not well developed then, but it is now. (The once lonely community of Heathcote, for example, is now Scarsdale's second town center and can boast some multimillion dollar homes.) The concept of public subsidy or ownership of commuter railroads did not exist then; it is now universal and has been for four decades. Nor was there such a thing as "railbanking"—that is, public acquisition of abandoned railroad rights-of-way to keep intact in case of future need. Now, finally, the Westchester is needed. Its final irony is that it was ahead of its time when built and ahead of a different kind of time when abandoned.

APPENDIX 1: ROSTER OF EQUIPMENT

Passenger Cars

All cars were electric steel multiple-unit coaches, except where noted. Equipped with two Westinghouse No. 409 or 409-B AC motors (145/175 hp each) carried on one truck; 57 mph balancing speed; WH AB control. Wheels 42" on motor truck and 36" on unpowered truck. Body length of all cars 70' 4"; length over buffers 72'; height, rail to rooftop, 13' 3.5"; body width 9' 7.75". Cars 101–40 and 191–95 originally had 78 seats, weight 120,000 lbs.; cars 141–80 had 80 seats, with varying weights: 141–50, 127,000 lbs.; 151–80, 126,900 lbs.; 181–90, 124,830 lbs. Air brakes: Electro-pneumatic, type AMCE.

101–28—Pressed Steel Car Co., 1911–12.

129–38—Pressed Steel, 1915.

139–40—Pressed Steel, 1912; rebuilt from combines 201–202 below in 1922.

141–50—Pressed Steel, 1924; owned by New Haven Railroad.

151–70—Pressed Steel, 1926; owned by New Haven Railroad.

171–80—Osgood-Bradley, 1927; owned by New Haven Railroad.

181–90—Osgood-Bradley, 1929; owned by New Haven Railroad.

191–95—Pressed Steel, 1915; rebuilt by NYW&B from trailers 501–505, c. 1929.

201–202—Pressed Steel, 1912; passenger-baggage combines; rebuilt to coaches 139–40 in 1922. Builder photo shows car numbered #01, but presumably renumbered soon thereafter.

501–505—Pressed Steel, 1915; control trailer coaches; motorized as Nos. 191–95 in 1928.

New Haven m.u. cars 4060–63 were leased to the NYW&B at various times in the 1932–34 period. Built by Standard Steel Car Co., 1915. These were AC-only cars formerly

All 95 NYW&B cars were virtually indistinguishable from one another, despite being built over a 16-year span. This set is laying over at Mamaroneck in 1927. Harry F. Brown photo, author's collection.

used in NH Harlem River branch local service. According to Arcara, five NH m.u. cars were leased to the NYW&B in this period while five Westchester cars were repaired at the NH's Van Nest electric shop.

Cars 141–90 were repossessed by the New Haven in 1938 and rebuilt for steam-powered suburban service out of Boston, carrying their original numbers. Rebuilding included removing headlights, installing steam lines, and modifying the carbodies to eliminate the center doors and provide additional seats. Twenty of these cars were sold in 1951 to ARAMCO for service in Saudi Arabia; others were retired and scrapped in the 1950s.

Car 122 was damaged in a runaway accident at Port Chester in 1936. It and two others that were damaged during the last years of operation were scrapped after service abandonment. The remaining 42 NYW&B–owned cars were sold 1942 to the U.S. Maritime Commission for use in Houston.

Freight and Work Equipment

01 (1911) to 301 (1914) to 701 (1928)—Baldwin-Westinghouse, 1911; B-B electric locomotive; 4-Westinghouse 410 AC motors (520/655 hp), multiple-unit control; weight 155,520 lbs.; 63" wheels; top speed 25 mph. Essentially identical to New Haven 0201–14 (EY-2) class, but slightly lighter. Became NH 0224, class EY-2c, in 1944; retired 1950.

No. 701 was the Westchester's sole power for freights, work trains, shop switching, emergency duties, and whatever else. Almost identical to the New Haven's large fleet of such switchers, it went to work for its parent in 1944. George Votava photo, September 1940, Bob's Photo collection.

Another jack-of-all-trades vehicle, gas-electric-powered No. 401 did the catenary maintenance work, but its 10-ton-capacity crane was also useful for track replacement jobs and clearing small mishaps. It helped build the Port Chester extension and scrap the system. George Votava photo, September 1940, Bob's Photo collection.

X-1 (1911) to 401 (1914)—Pressed Steel–General Electric, 1911; gas-electric line car-crane; scrapped c. 1942.

1–4—40′ work flatcars, Pressed Steel, 1911; No. 4 had a wood shelter structure added 1915 to serve as a combination work car-caboose.

4—40′ work car-caboose, as above.

5—40′ work boxcar, Pressed Steel, 1911; wood body, steel underframe and floor; rebuilt as a mobile machine shop car equipped with pantograph and transformer to power machine tools inside.

NH C-136—New Haven wood caboose, periodically leased by NYW&B.

Note: Electric motor horsepower is shown at continuous rating (the lower figure) and short-term (hourly) rating.

Sources: Electric Railway Journal, March 30, 1912, and subsequent car order details in vol. 67 (1926): 1130; vol. 68 (1927): 1213; vol. 71 (1928): 235, 683; vol. 72 (1928): 244; Arcara, *Westchester's Forgotten Railway,* 75–76; Bang, *The New York, Westchester & Boston Railway Company, 1906–1946,* 78; Groh, "New York, Westchester & Boston Railway," 8; Swanberg, *New Haven Power,* 312, 338, 415.

APPENDIX 2: NYW&B STATION LIST

Mileages shown are from Harlem River terminal.
All stations owned by NYW&B were built 1911–12 unless noted.
(L) = Local station.
(E) = Express station.
(Except in rush hours, all stations north and east of Columbus Avenue, Mount Vernon, were local stations.)
Trolley connections shown as of 1915. The New York & Stamford car line was nearby between Larchmont and Mamaroneck until 1927; afterward, County Transportation buses connected at joint NYW&B–New Haven stations between Larchmont and Port Chester.

0.0—Harlem River (East 132nd/133rd Street): Original four-story terminal building (which included NH offices) built c. 1901–1902, replacing an 1891 structure; burned and replaced by a similar building in 1922. New terminal built for NYW&B and remaining NH local services in 1924. New Haven interlocking tower SS1 NE of station. Connection to IRT Third Avenue elevated; Third Avenue Ry. Southern Blvd. trolley a block away.

1.2—Port Morris, Bronx (L): New Haven station built 1908; Third Avenue Ry. 138th Street Crosstown trolley connection.

2.3—Casanova, Bronx (L): New Haven station, built c. 1909; Third Avenue Ry. Southern Blvd. trolley connection.

2.4—New Haven Oak Point (Casanova) interlocking SS4, controlling crossovers and entry to Oak Point yard, used by NYW&B freights.

2.8—Hunt's Point, Bronx (E), New Haven station, built 1908; connection to IRT subway; Third Avenue Ry. 163rd Street Crosstown and Southern Blvd. trolley connections.

3.2—Westchester Avenue, Bronx (L), New Haven station, built 1908; three Third Avenue Ry. trolley lines.

3.75—West Farms Junction (East 174th Street, Bronx), junction with New Haven Harlem River Branch, beginning of NYW&B property. No station. New Haven interlocking tower SS8 on west side of line. Junction was reconfigured several times, and NH–NYW&B switches removed and interlocking closed November 1931.

4.4—East 180th Street, Bronx (E), station and NYW&B general office building; interlocking in rear of station complex; connection to IRT subway and three Third Avenue Ry. trolley lines.

5.6—Morris Park, Bronx (L).

5.9—Pelham Parkway, Bronx (E) (in subway section).

6.85—Gun Hill Road, Bronx (L).

7.6—Baychester Avenue, Bronx (L); BY interlocking tower SW of station, controlling three crossovers. Crossovers removed and tower closed sometime before 1930.

8.4—Dyre Avenue, Bronx (L); Westchester Electric RR South Fifth Avenue (Mount Vernon) trolley connection.

8.7—Kingsbridge Road, Mount Vernon (L).

9.3—East Sixth Street, Mount Vernon (L); freight station and team track SE of station; Westchester Electric RR Fulton Avenue–Sixth Street trolleys.

9.8—East Third Street, Mount Vernon (E) Westchester Electric RR trolley connection.

10.3—Columbus Avenue, Mount Vernon (L); connection to New Haven station below.

10.5—Columbus Avenue Junction; CA interlocking tower; junction of New Rochelle/Port Chester and White Plains branches. No station.

New Rochelle and Port Chester Branch

11.0—Fifth Avenue, North Pelham; Westchester Electric RR North Pelham trolley connection.

11.3—Pelhamwood, New Rochelle (originally called Clifford).

11.7—Webster Avenue, New Rochelle (originally called Remington Place); Westchester Electric RR Webster Avenue trolley connection.

12.2—North Avenue, New Rochelle; NR interlocking tower at SW end of station; dual passing tracks west of station (both later dead-ended); Westchester Electric RR Tuckahoe and Fifth Avenue trolleys.

12.35—Larchmont Junction, located at the point east of North Avenue station where the NYW&B met the New Haven mainline. Track connection and NH tower, built c. 1911–12; connection and tower removed c. 1920.

13.0—Pine Brook, New Rochelle, built for NYW&B only use, 1921.

14.03—Larchmont, New Haven–NYW&B joint station, built 1887–88; N.Y. & Stamford Larchmont Manor branch trolley connection (1921–27).

14.8—Larchmont Gardens, built for NYW&B only use, 1926.

15.8—Mamaroneck, New Haven–NYW&B joint station, built 1887–88.

16.8—West Street, Harrison, built for NYW&B only use, 1927.

17.6—Harrison, New Haven–NYW&B joint station, Harrison Avenue, built 1886–87.

19.44—Rye, New Haven–NYW&B joint station, built 1888; new addition built c. 1927–28. County Transportation Rye Beach bus connection, 1928.

20.9—Port Chester (Westchester Avenue), built in 1929 for NYW&B use only. NYW&B PC interlocking tower SW of station. County Transportation bus connections, 1929–37.

White Plains Branch

10.7—East Lincoln Avenue, Mount Vernon; Westchester Electric RR North Pelham–Tuckahoe trolley connections.

11.7—Chester Heights, Eastchester; Westchester Electric RR Pelham–Mount Vernon trolley connection.

13.1—Wykagyl, New Rochelle; WY interlocking tower NW of station; dual passing tracks in station (both later dead-ended); freight station and team track NW of station; Westchester Electric RR New Rochelle–Tuckahoe trolley connection.

15.15—Quaker Ridge, New Rochelle.

16.0—Heathcote, Scarsdale; HC interlocking tower NW of station; dual passing sidings in station (both later dead-ended); freight station west of passenger station.

17.51—Ridgeway, White Plains, built 1926.

18.3—Gedney Way, White Plains; not built when the railroad opened in 1912, but completed c. 1913–14. Team track SW of station.

18.9—Mamaroneck Avenue, White Plains; Westchester Street RR White Plains–Mamaroneck trolley connection.

19.5—Westchester Avenue terminal, White Plains; freight station, team tracks, and yard west of station; WP interlocking tower SE of station; Westchester Street RR Westchester Avenue–Silver Lake trolley connection.

In New York Harbor, the NYW&B advertised that it received freight at the New Haven's Pier 45 (later 37), East River (at Montgomery Street), and until about 1927 at Pier 70 East River, at the foot of 23rd Street. Freight was also received at an NH facility on the Harlem River at 132nd Street and Lincoln Avenue, west of the passenger terminal. There was only one official tariff freight interchange point, shown as with the New Haven at the West Farms–174th Street junction, although cars were not physically interchanged there. The actual physical interchange point was the New Haven's carfloat terminal and yard at Oak Point in the Bronx.

Sources: NYW&B station lists; passenger timetables for 1915 and 1937; Bang, *The New York, Westchester & Boston Railway Company, 1906–1946,* 54–64; and the *Official Guide of the Railways,* June 1916, February 1926, and February 1928.

NOTES

1. Before the Beginning

1. This summary of the New York & Harlem's early history is taken from Carl W. Condit, *The Port of New York* (Chicago: University of Chicago Press, 1980), 1:23–26; Louis V. Grogan, *The Coming of the New York and Harlem Railroad* (Pawling, N.Y.: privately published, 1989), 2–14; and Alvin F. Harlow, *The Road of the Century* (New York: Creative Age Press, 1947), 119–25.

2. Condit, *Port of New York,* 1:29–30.

3. Harlow, *Road of the Century,* 195.

4. Edward Hungerford, *Men and Iron: The History of New York Central* (New York: Thomas Y. Crowell, 1938), 131; Richard F. Crandell, *This Is Westchester* (New York: Sterling, 1954), 42.

5. For the full history of the New York City & Northern–New York Central Putnam Division, see Daniel R. Gallo and Frederick A. Kramer, *The Putnam Division: New York Central's Bygone Route through Westchester County* (New York: Quadrant Press, 1981).

6. Alvin F. Harlow, *Steelways of New England* (New York: Creative Age Press, 1946), 193.

7. L. S. Miller's report, Interstate Commerce Commission, *Investigation of the Financial Affairs of the New Haven Railroad,* 2:2289 (hereafter referred to as the *ICC Investigation*). The spelling of the eastern terminal of the branch in the Bronx was also given as Throgg's Neck. The name honored an immigrant English farmer named John Throgmorton.

8. Ibid., 2:2290.

9. Stephen Jenkins, *The Story of the Bronx* (New York: G. P. Putnam's Sons, 1912), 242; Jack W. Swanberg, *New Haven Power, 1838–1968* (Medina, Ohio: Alvin F. Staufer, 1988), 80; *Railway Age Gazette,* January 28 and February 4, 1910.

10. William D. Middleton, *Metropolitan Railways: Rapid Transit in America* (Bloomington: Indiana University Press, 2003), 38–42.

11. See Condit, *Port of New York,* 1:118–28.

12. William D. Middleton, *When the Steam Railroads Electrified* (Milwaukee: Kalmbach Books, 1974), 38, 74–79.

13. Census population figures quoted in *Electric Railway Journal,* May 25, 1912, 865. (Note: Some issues of the *Electric Railway Journal* and other railroad publications will be listed here using dates, and the rest will be listed by volume number. This was the way that the author recorded them in the early 1950s.)

14. John L. Weller, *The New Haven Railroad: Its Rise and Fall* (New York: Hastings House, 1969), 6.

15. Ibid., 40.

16. Ibid., 45–48.

17. Ibid., 49–50.

18. See, e.g., Jean Strouse, *Morgan: American Financier* (New York: Random House, 1999), 616, 662–63.

2. A Deep Fog Descends

1. *ICC Investigation,* 1:45. The spelling of the railroad's name and terminal city seems to alternate by the writer's whim between "Port Chester" and "Portchester," with the two-word form being official.

2. Details of the New York & Port Chester project are covered in the *Street Railway Journal* 18 (1901): 81, 829; *Railroad Gazette* 34 (1902): 331; and Jenkins, *Story of the Bronx,* 247–48.

3. Weller, *New Haven Railroad,* 100.

4. *Railroad Gazette* 34 (1902): 332.

5. *ICC Investigation,* 1:4.

6. New York, Westchester & Boston Ry., *Prospectus, First Mortgage Five Per Cent. Gold Bonds,* Dick & Robinson, Bankers, New York, 1904; *ICC Investigation,* 1:44, 2:2290; Weller, *New Haven Railroad,* 100; *New York Times,* January 13, 1904.

7. New York, Westchester & Boston Ry., *Prospectus; New York Times,* January 13, 1904.

8. *Wall Street Summary,* April 1, 1905.

9. *New York Post,* March 16, 1904.

10. *ICC Investigation,* 2:2292.

11. Weller, *New Haven Railroad,* 100–101; New York City, Bureau of Municipal Investigation and Statistics, Department of Finance, *Accounting of Disbursements of the New York, Westchester and Boston Railway Company from August 2, 1904, to August 2, 1906, for Purposes Other than Purchase of Right of Way,* New York, October 5, 1906, 48–51.

12. New York City, Bureau of Municipal Investigation and Statistics, *Accounting of Disbursements,* 4–8, 12–15; NYW&B, *New York Rapid Transit* (brochure), 1906, 15. For photos of bridgework construction in this period, see Robert Bang, *The New York, Westchester & Boston Railway Company, 1906–1946* (Port Chester, N.Y.: privately published, 2004), 29–31.

13. Roger Arcara, *Westchester's Forgotten Railway,* 3rd ed. (New Rochelle, N.Y.: I&T, 1985), 11, 137.

14. Weller, *New Haven Railroad,* 62–63, 101–102; Strouse, *Morgan,* 594. Perry biography from http://www.redwoodlibrary.org/notables/perry.htm.

15. Weller, *New Haven Railroad,* 101–102.

16. C. S. Mellen testimony, *ICC Investigation,* 1:4, 723–26.

17. Oakleigh Thorne testimony, *ICC Investigation,* 1:52, 212.

18. *ICC Investigation,* 1:52; *New York Times,* October 30, 1907.

19. Mellen testimony, *ICC Investigation,* 1:728.

20. Ibid., 727.

21. Ibid., 732.

22. Ibid., 730.

23. Thorne's testimony, *ICC Investigation,* 1:226.

24. Ibid., 214.
25. Weller, *New Haven Railroad,* 112.
26. NYNH&H, annual statement for year ending June 30, 1908.

3. Building the Perfect Railroad

1. *ICC Investigation,* 1:6.
2. These events are related in detail in Mellen's testimony, *ICC Investigation,* 1:698–711, and summarized at 1:6–7.
3. *Biographical Directory of Railroad Officials of America* (Chicago: Railway Age, 1906; New York: Simmons-Boardman, 1922); *ICC Investigation,* 1:237.
4. William D. Middleton, *Grand Central: The World's Greatest Railway Terminal* (San Marino, Calif.: Golden West Books, 1977), 63–66.
5. Author's interview with Alfred Fellheimer, 1953. Following Charles Reed's death in November 1911, Reed & Stem was re-formed as Stem & Fellheimer, then as Fellheimer & Wagner. During his earlier career, Fellheimer designed many landmark stations for the New York Central and other railroads, including the Buffalo Central Terminal and the magnificent 1933 art deco Cincinnati Union Terminal.
6. See Harry Hansen, *Scarsdale: From Colonial Manor to Modern Community* (New York: Harper & Brothers, 1954), 9–13.
7. Fellheimer interview. For photos of Westchester construction in the 1910–12 period, see Bang, *NYW&B Company,* 9–28, 31–36.
8. As noted in the text, the Westchester was the toast of the technical trade magazines at the time, and various 1912 issues of such publications as *Electric Railway Journal, Engineering News, Electric Journal, Electric Traction, Technical World,* and *Railway Age Gazette* carried extensive articles on its construction, infrastructure, and rolling stock. The most detailed are in *Electric Railway Journal,* May 25 and June 8, 1912 (and other issues as noted elsewhere); *Engineering News,* 1913, 1153; *Technical World,* February 1913, 719–21; *Railway Age Gazette,* June 7, 1912; and *ICC Investigation,* 2:1227. Several of the most detailed articles were reprinted in Roger Arcara's *Westchester's Forgotten Railroad* and in a predecessor volume, *When the Westchester Was New* (New York: Electric Railroaders Association, 1964). As of 2007, some of this material was also available at http://www.nycsubway.org/nyc/nywb.
9. For full details on the Westchester electrification, see *Electric Railway Journal,* June 15, 1912; for the West Farms feeder, see *Electric Railway Journal,* December 18, 1915, 1200–1204.
10. For full technical details on the Westchester's signal and communications systems, see *Electric Railway Journal,* July 20, 1912. See also Michael Weinman, "A History of the New York, Westchester & Boston Railway," thesis, New York University, 1965, 33.
11. See *Electric Railway Journal,* March 30, 1912, for technical details of the NYW&B multiple-unit cars. Other trade publications also described the cars in detail. For data on the NYW&B's locomotive, see Swanberg, *New Haven Power,* 312, 338. Data on the gas-electric line car appeared in *Electric Railway Journal,* June 15, 1912.
12. *Electric Railway Journal,* June 8, 1912, 956.
13. See *Railway Age Gazette,* January 28 and February 4, 1910.
14. For technical details on the Westchester stations, see *Electric Railway Journal,* June 8, 1912.
15. See *Electric Railway Journal,* December 14, 1912.

4. Running the Railroad

1. Arcara, *Westchester's Forgotten Railway,* 14.
2. Weinman, "History," 10–11.

3. Ibid., 44.

4. Ibid., 44–45; New York, Westchester & Boston Railway timetable, June 6, 1915.

5. Weinman, "History," 45–46; Karl Groh, "The New York, Westchester & Boston Railway," *ERA Electric Railroads No. 31*, April 1962, 11. Kreschollek quote from piercehavilland.com, online.

6. Weinman, "History," 37.

7. Running times and mileages from NYW&B passenger timetable, January 3, 1937.

8. Weinman, "History," 56–59, 77–78.

9. New York, Westchester & Boston Railway, *Facts Worth Knowing about the Bronx and Westchester County,* real estate promotional folder, New York, c. 1912, in J. W. Swanberg collection; baggage handling station detail from New York, Westchester & Boston Railway, Passenger Tariff, Harlem River–White Plains, July 1, 1929.

10. Weinman, "History," 47.

11. Crandell, *This Is Westchester,* 112.

12. For a fully detailed listing of New York subway opening dates, see Herman Rinke, "New York Subways: Fifty Years of Millions!" *ERA Electric Railroads No. 23,* October 1954; see also Stan Fischler, *The Subway: A Trip through Time on New York's Rapid Transit* (Flushing, N.Y.: H&M Productions, 1997), 239.

13. Hansen, *Scarsdale,* 96, 142–43.

14. *Transit Journal,* December 1937, 492; Arcara, *Westchester's Forgotten Railway,* 23.

15. *Technical World,* February 1913, 719.

16. *ICC Investigation,* 1:9–10.

17. *Electric Railway Journal,* June 1, 1912, 901.

5. But Why?

1. Henry Lee Staples and Alpheus T. Mason, *The Fall of a Railroad Empire: Brandeis and the New Haven Merger Battle* (Syracuse, N.Y.: Syracuse University Press, 1947), 18; Weller, *New Haven Railroad,* 131–32.

2. Staples and Mason, *Fall,* 24–36.

3. Ibid., 95–97; Weller, *New Haven Railroad,* 149–50.

4. Staples and Mason, *Fall,* 148; Weller, *New Haven Railroad,* 157.

5. Weller, *New Haven Railroad,* 168.

6. Staples and Mason, *Fall,* 122.

7. *ICC Investigation,* 2:1239–40, quoting from Boston investigation, 26–30.

8. Staples and Mason, *Fall,* 164; Weller, *New Haven Railroad,* 172–75.

9. Mellen testimony, *ICC Investigation,* 1:749.

10. *ICC Investigation,* 1:4, 10.

11. Author's interview with Professor Healy, 1953.

12. *Engineering News* 71 (1914): 1206.

13. Strouse, *Morgan,* 615–16.

14. Frederick Lewis Allen, *The Great Pierpont Morgan* (New York: Harper & Brothers, 1949), 237.

15. See *Electric Railway Journal,* February 26, 1912, 334, 355. The rationale is discussed in far more detail in *ICC Investigation,* 1:287, 291, 2:2294–2306, 2314–15; Massachusetts Public Service Commission, *Report on the Capital Expenditures, Investments, and Existing Contingent Liabilities of the New York, New Haven & Hartford Railroad Co.,* House no. 1900, 1916, 242–43.

6. The Phantom Westchester Northern

1. Incorporation papers of the Mt. Vernon & Eastern Railroad, Westchester County, N.Y., Archives, Elmsford, N.Y., file A-0050(18), p. 275; *Report of the Joint Commission on the Assets and*

Liabilities of the New York, New Haven & Hartford Railroad Co., [Massachusetts], February 15, 1911, 500.

    2. *ICC Investigation,* 2:2301; *Poor's Railroad Manual,* 1913 ed., 20; Westchester County incorporation records. See also Weller, *New Haven Railroad,* 100.

    3. Tom Curtin, "The Berkshire Line," *Shoreliner* 10, no. 3 (1979): 6–19.

    4. NYW&B internal tax memo, November 24, 1937, as reproduced in Bang, *NYW&B Company, 1906–1946,* 175; letter from E. E. Oviatt, chief engineer, NYNH&H RR, to Allison Albee, Rye, N.Y., April 19, 1945, in J. W. Swanberg collection.

    5. *Poor's Railroad Manual,* 1917 ed., 878–79; *New York Times,* November 8, 1912.

    6. NYNH&H, annual statement, 1913.

    7. *Travelers' Official Guide of the Railways,* June 1870, listing No. 76.

    8. Data on the NYH&N and Southern Westchester from Gregg M. Turner and Melancthon W. Jacobus, *Connecticut Railroads: An Illustrated History* (Hartford: Connecticut Historical Society, 1986), 54–55; Arcara, *Westchester's Forgotten Railway,* 9; Bang, *NYW&B Company,* 3–4; Oviatt to Albee, April 19, 1945.

7. Making the Best of Life

    1. NYNH&H, annual statement, June 30, 1913; *Wall Street Journal,* February 1, 1913.

    2. NYNH&H, annual statements, 1913–29; Weller, *New Haven Railroad,* 188.

    3. Interborough Rapid Transit Company, annual report, 1917; Rinke, "Fifty Years of Millions!" 2.

    4. Weinman, "History," 24; Arcara, *Westchester's Forgotten Railway,* 21.

    5. See *New York Times,* September 2, 1923, and April 13, 1924.

    6. *Poor's Railroad Manual,* 1925 ed., 571; *Electric Railway Journal,* March 9, 1924.

    7. Opening dates from *Poor's Railroad Manual,* 1937 ed., 2373.

    8. See Arcara, *Westchester's Forgotten Railway,* 57.

    9. NYNH&H, annual statement, 1926; Arcara, *Westchester's Forgotten Railway,* 15–16, 46.

    10. Hansen, *Scarsdale,* 96; G. M. Hopkins & Co., *Atlas of Westchester County, 1930.* Under various names, the Donnybrook Lodge became a popular spot for local social occasions, and today it is on Westchester County's historic structures register.

    11. Hansen, *Scarsdale,* 96; *New York Times,* May 3, June 3, June 5, and June 8, 1930.

    12. Harold M. Lewis, *Report on the Proposal to Extend the New York, Westchester & Boston Railway to 125th Street, Manhattan,* 6; reproduced in Bang, *NYW&B Company,* 158.

    13. Vincent F. Seyfried, *Roster of Equipment: Third Avenue Railway System, 1853–1953* (privately published, 1953), 102; *McGraw Electric Railway Directory* (New York: McGraw-Hill, 1924), item nos. 549 (N.Y. & Stamford) and 570 (Westchester Street R.R.).

    14. *Electric Railway Journal* 66 (1925): 142, 415; 67 (1926): 737; 69 (1927): 752; 70 (1927): 448; 73 (1929): 808; Weinman, "History," 67–69; *Poor's Railroad Manual,* 1933 ed., 953; 1936, 1117.

    15. Seyfried, *Roster of Equipment,* 102.

    16. Weinman, "History," 67; Groh, "The New York, Westchester & Boston Railway," 14; NYNH&H, annual statement, 1927; correspondence from Bernard Linder, New York area traction historian, March 7, 2007.

    17. Weinman, "History," 69; Linder correspondence.

    18. *Bus Transportation,* January 1928, 1; *Electric Railway Journal* 73 (1929): 808.

    19. *Poor's Railroad Manual,* 1936 ed., 1117; 1939 ed., 952; Weinman, "History," 67.

    20. Linder correspondence.

    21. Suburban Transit Engineering Board, *Progress Report on Suburban Transit for the Metropolitan District of New York,* 1930, 19.

    22. *New York Times,* October 1, 1925.

    23. *Journal of Commerce,* February 5, 1926; Lewis, *Report.*

24. Westchester County Transit Commission, *Final Report of the Westchester County Transit Commission to the Board of Supervisors of Westchester County, Containing an Engineering Report on Westchester Suburban Transit by Henry M. Brinckerhoff,* New York, March 1, 1926.

25. New Haven Railroad annual reports, 1913, 1923, 1928; Lewis, *Report,* 6, reproduced in Bang, *NYW&B Company,* 158; Weinman, "History," 48.

26. Weinman, "History," 72.

27. New Haven Railroad, annual statements, 1913–29.

8. Down and Out (I): Down

1. *New York Times,* October 28, 1928.
2. New York State Transit Commission, annual reports, 1930, 1931; New Haven Railroad, annual reports, 1929–1933.
3. Weller, *New Haven Railroad,* 199.
4. *Poor's Railroad Manual,* 1930 ed., 602.
5. *New York Times,* August 29, 1930.
6. New Haven Railroad, annual statements, 1935.
7. "From Nowhere to Nowhere," *Time,* October 25, 1937, 64.
8. New Haven Railroad, annual statement, 1935.
9. *Railway Age* 103 (1937): 176.
10. *New York Times,* June 6, 1936.
11. *New York Times,* January 25, 1936.
12. *New York Times,* May 29, 1936.
13. *Poor's Railroad Manual,* 1938 ed., 619.
14. *New York Times,* June 5 and June 6, 1936.
15. Author's interview with James L. Dohr, the Westchester's last receiver, 1953.
16. *New York Times,* August 22, 1936.
17. Dohr interview.
18. Dohr interview; *Transit Journal,* December 1937, 493.
19. *New York Times,* September 2, 1936.
20. United States District Court for the District of Connecticut, *Plan of Reorganization of the New York, Westchester & Boston Ry. Co., Proposed by the First Mortgage Bondholders Protective Committee,* New York, December 19, 1936.
21. *Transit Journal,* December 1937, 493.
22. *New York Times,* January 1, 1937.
23. J. William Vigrass, "A Train That Never Was," *New Electric Railway Journal,* Summer 1991.
24. *Transit Journal,* December 1937, 492.
25. New Haven Railroad, annual statement, 1936.

9. Down and Out (II): Out

1. *New York Times,* April 4, 1937; *Railway Age,* May 1, 1937, 774.
2. Dohr interview.
3. *New York Times,* June 29, 1937; *Poor's Railroad Manual,* 1938 ed., 2435.
4. *New York Times,* July 7, 1937.
5. *Railway Age* 103 (1937): 176.
6. Dohr interview.
7. *Transit Journal,* December 1937, 494.

8. *New York Times,* October 18, 1937; *Railway Age,* October 23, 1937, 587; *Railway Age* 103 (December 4, 1937): 810; Weinman, "History," 91.

9. *Transit Journal,* December 1937, 493.

10. *New York Times,* November 2, 1937.

11. *Railway Age* 103 (December 4, 1937): 810.

12. *New York Times,* December 18, 1937; *Railway Age* 103 (1937): 926.

13. *New York Times,* January 1, 1938; Weinman, "History," 93; Groh, "The New York, Westchester & Boston Railway," 3.

14. New Haven Railroad, annual statement, 1937; Weinman, "History," 95.

15. *Railway Age* 104 (1938): 354.

16. *Railway Age* 104 (1938): 424.

17. *Railway Age* 104 (March 26, 1938): 517.

18. *Railway Age,* April 23, 1938, 744.

19. *Railway Age,* April 23, 1938, 744; *Poor's Railroad Manual,* 1938 ed., 620.

20. *New York Times,* November 6, 1938.

21. *New York Times,* May 30, 1939.

22. *Business Week,* November 15, 1941, 79.

23. *New York Times,* April 7 and May 2, 1939.

24. *Poor's Railroad Manual,* 1939 ed., 950; *New York Times,* May 30, 1939.

25. *Poor's Railroad Manual,* 1940 ed., 877.

26. *Railway Age* 108 (May 4, 1940): 791.

27. *Moody's Railroad Manual, 1941,* 1170–71; *Moody's Railroad Manual, 1942,* 911.

28. *New York Times,* May 16, 1941.

29. *Railway Age,* May 24, 1941, 956; Arcara, *Westchester's Forgotten Railway,* 43; Brian J. Cudahy, *Under the Sidewalks of New York* (Brattleboro, Vt.: Stephen Greene Press, 1979), 110–11.

30. *Railway Age* 112 (April 25, 1942): 828; roster in Groh, "The New York, Westchester & Boston Railway," 8, reproduced in Bang, *NYW&B Company,* 174.

31. Weinman, "History," 100–101.

BIBLIOGRAPHY

Books

Abrams, Richard M. "Brandeis and the New Haven-Boston & Maine Merger Battle Revisited." *Business History Review* 36, no. 4 (Winter 1962).

Allen, Frederick Lewis. *The Great Pierpont Morgan.* New York: Harper & Brothers, 1949.

Arcara, Roger. *Westchester's Forgotten Railway: An Account of the New York, Westchester & Boston Railway.* 3rd ed. New Rochelle, N.Y.: I&T, 1985.

Bang, Robert A. *The New York, Westchester & Boston Railway Company, 1906–1946.* Port Chester, N.Y.: privately published, 2004.

———. *Westchester County's Million-Dollar-a-Mile Railroad, 1912–1937.* Port Chester, N.Y.: privately published, n.d.

Condit, Carl W. *The Port of New York.* 2 vols. Chicago: University of Chicago Press, 1980, 1981.

Crandell, Richard F. *This Is Westchester.* New York: Sterling, 1954.

Cudahy, Brian J. *Under the Sidewalks of New York.* Brattleboro, Vt.: Stephen Greene Press, 1979.

Curtin, Tom. "The Berkshire Line." *Shoreliner* 10, no. 3 (1979): 6–19. New Haven Railroad Historical & Technical Association; address varies, but may be reached online at www.nhrhta.org.

Fischler, Stan. *The Subway: A Trip through Time on New York's Rapid Transit.* Flushing, N.Y.: H&M Productions, 1997.

Grogan, Louis V. *The Coming of the New York & Harlem Railroad.* Pawling, N.Y.: privately published, 1989.

Groh, Karl. "New York, Westchester & Boston Railway." *ERA Electric Railroads No. 31,* April 1962.

Hansen, Harry. *Scarsdale: From Colonial Manor to Modern Community.* New York: Harper & Brothers, 1954.

Harlow, Alvin F. *Steelways of New England.* New York: Creative Age Press, 1946.

———. *The Road of the Century.* New York: Creative Age Press, 1947.

Harwood, Herbert H., Jr. "The New York, Westchester and Boston Railway: A Transportation Tragedy." Thesis, Princeton University, 1953.

Hungerford, Edward. *Men and Iron: The History of New York Central.* New York: Thomas Y. Crowell, 1938.

Jenkins, Steven. *The Story of the Bronx.* New York: G. P. Putnam's Sons, 1912.

Lewis, Harold M. *Report on the Proposal to Extend the New York, Westchester & Boston Railway to 125th Street, Manhattan.* Commissioned by Harlem Board of Commerce, New York, 1929.

Macey, Barry A. "Charles Sanger Mellen: Architect of Transportation Monopoly." *Historical New Hampshire* 26, no. 4 (Winter 1971).

Massachusetts Public Utilities Commission. *Report on the Capital Expenditures, Investments, and Existing Contingent Liabilities of the New York, New Haven & Hartford Railroad Co.* House no. 1900. Boston, 1916. A summary of previous investigations on this subject, with some new findings and conclusions. Much space is devoted to the Westchester affair.

McGraw Electric Railway Directory, 1924. New York: McGraw-Hill, 1924.

Middleton, William D. *When the Steam Railroads Electrified.* Milwaukee: Kalmbach Books, 1974.

———. *Grand Central: The World's Greatest Railway Terminal.* San Marino, Calif.: Golden West Books, 1977.

———. *Metropolitan Railways: Rapid Transit in America.* Bloomington: Indiana University Press, 2003.

New York City, Bureau of Municipal Investigation and Statistics, Department of Finance. *Accounting of Disbursements of the New York, Westchester and Boston Railway Company from August 2, 1904, to August 2, 1906, for Purposes Other than Purchase of Right of Way.* New York, October 5, 1906. Details construction expenditures in this period.

Report of the Joint Commission on the Assets and Liabilities of the New York, New Haven & Hartford Railroad Co. [Massachusetts]. February 15, 1911. Boston: Wright and Potter Printing Co., State Printers, 1911.

Rinke, Herman. "New York Subways: Fifty Years of Millions!" *ERA Electric Railroads No. 23.* October 1954.

Seyfried, Vincent F. *Roster of Equipment: Third Avenue Railway System, 1853–1953.* Privately published, 1953.

Staples, Henry Lee, and Alpheus T. Mason. *The Fall of a Railroad Empire: Brandeis and the New Haven Merger Battle.* Syracuse, N.Y.: Syracuse University Press, 1947.

State of New York Transit Commission. Annual reports. Albany, N.Y., 1921–38. Financial and operating statistics of all street, rapid transit, and suburban railways in the New York City area.

Strouse, Jean. *Morgan: American Financier.* New York: Random House, 1999.

Suburban Transit Engineering Board. *Progress Report on Suburban Transit for the Metropolitan District of New York.* New York, 1930. This contains studies by the Port Authority of New York on suburban traffic, destinations, etc., plus recommendations for the future.

Swanberg, Jack W. *New Haven Power, 1838–1968.* Medina, Ohio: A. F. Staufer, 1988.

Turner, Gregg M., and Melancthon W. Jacobus. *Connecticut Railroads: An Illustrated History.* Hartford: Connecticut Historical Society, 1986.

United States District Court for the District of Connecticut. *Plan of Reorganization of the New York, Westchester & Boston Ry. Co., Proposed by the First Mortgage Bondholders Protective Committee.* December 19, 1936. The so-called Sartorius Committee's first reorganization plan, referred to in chapter 9.

United States Interstate Commerce Commission. *Evidence Taken before the Interstate Commerce Commission Relative to Financial Transactions of the New York, New Haven & Hartford Railroad Co.* 2 vols. Document no. 543. 63rd Congress, 1914. Testimony, evidence, and the ICC's conclusions from the 1914 hearings. This is the best source for the NYW&B's early history and the financial dealings leading to its construction.

Vigrass, J. William. "A Train That Never Was." *New Electric Railway Journal,* Summer 1991.

Weinman, Michael. "A History of the New York, Westchester and Boston Railway." Thesis, New York University, 1965.

Weller, John L. *The New Haven Railroad: Its Rise and Fall.* New York: Hastings House, 1969.
Westchester County Transit Commission. *Final Report of the Westchester County Transit Commission to the Board of Supervisors of Westchester County, Containing an Engineering Report on Westchester Suburban Transit by Henry M. Brinckerhoff.* New York, March 1, 1926. This report, drawn up by Parsons, Klapp, Brinckerhoff, & Douglas, concerns various proposals to alleviate the New York terminal situation, including a projected subway for suburban railroads into Manhattan.

Financial Manuals, Annual Reports, and Directories

Biographical Directory of Railway Officials of America. Chicago: Railway Age Co. (1906 ed.) and New York: Simmons-Boardman (1922 ed.). See also *Who's Who in Railroading,* this publication's later title.

Interborough Rapid Transit Co. Annual reports. New York, 1916–20.

Moody's Railroad Manual. New York: Moody's Investors Service, 1941, 1942.

New York, New Haven & Hartford Railroad Co. Annual statements. New Haven, Conn., 1907–38.

Official Guide of the Railways. New York: Railway Equipment Publishing Co., various monthly issues, 1916–37.

Poor's Public Utilities Manual. New York: Poor's Manual Co., 1929–40.

Poor's Railroad Manual. New York: Poor's Manual Co., 1912–40.

Travelers' Official Guide of the Railways. Philadelphia: National Railway, June 1, 1870.

Who's Who in Railroading. New York: Simmons-Boardman, 1930.

Miscellaneous Publications

Guaranty Trust Co. of New York, letter to holders of New York, Westchester & Boston Ry. Co. 1st Mortgage Gold Bonds, October 19, 1936.

New York, Westchester & Boston Railway Co. *New York Rapid Transit.* New York, 1906. An illustrated brochure of the original (1904) NYW&B project, including maps, photographs, and plans for the enterprise.

New York, Westchester & Boston Railway Co. *Facts Worth Knowing about the Bronx and Westchester County.* Real estate promotional folder, c. 1912. J. W. Swanberg collection.

New York, Westchester & Boston Railway Co. Passenger timetables, various issues, 1915–37.

INDEX

Italicized page numbers indicate illustrations.

accidents, runaway, 132
Adams Express Co., 60–61
Aldrich, Sen. Nelson W., 25
Allen, Frederick Lewis, 74–75
Anheuser-Busch Brewing Co., 68
architecture: Donnybrook Lodge, 97, *98*; 1887–1888 stations, *93, 94*; later style, 89, 95–97; ornaments, 44, *54, 55*; station design, 43–44, *47–56*, 92; towers, *53, 56, 96, 128*. See also Alfred Fellheimer; Cass Gilbert
Arnold, C. E., 84

B. J. Van Ingen & Co., 124
banking, "Panic of 1907," 26–27, 28
banks in railroad transactions, 25, 26–27
Bardo, Clinton L., 108–13, 117
Barney, Charles T., 25, 26
Berle, Adolf A., 122
Boston, Hartford & Erie RR, 84
Boston (Mass.) plans, 80, 84
Boston & Maine RR, 14, 17, 71, 88
Brandeis, Louis D., 71–72
Brewster, N.Y., *78*, 79–80, 100
bridges, New Haven RR: Bronx River, *104*; Hell Gate, 34, *120*
bridges, NY&PRR: Harrison, 25
bridges, NYW&B, 5, 35; construction of, *30*; overpasses, *24*, 24–25, *38, 90*; trestles, 5, *30, 36, 37, 107*

Bronx, N.Y., 12; East 180th St. service, 57–58; 1906 construction, *24*, 24–25; NYW&B right-of-way analysis, 122; overpasses, *24*, 24–25, *90*; rail connections in, 88–89; West Farms junction, *41, 121*. See also Bronx terminals
Bronx right-of-way, sale of, 124
Bronx River Parkway, 105
Bronx terminals, 43; Baychester Ave., *126*; East 180th St., 43, *47*, 125, *126, 127*; freight handling, 60–61; Hunt's Point, *55*, 135; list of (*see* appendix 2); location drawbacks, 75; Tremont, *12*; Westchester Ave., *49*; Woodlawn, *13*. See also Harlem River terminal
Brookfield, Conn., 84
Budd, Edward G., 114
Bull, William Lanman, 20
buses: connections to (*see* appendix 2); NYW&B, 99–101
business, NYW&B: analysis of, 68–69, 71–76; collapse of, 106–108; Depression era, 106–15; effects on automobiles, 105–106; franchises, 24–25, 57; freight (*see* freight business: NYW&B); reorganization attempts, 113–15; repossession of, 117–20, 122–24, 125–27; shared with NYNH&H, 99–101. See also finances, NYW&B
business corruption, 24, 25, 31–32, 71–72. See also J. Pierpont Morgan: secret acquisitions
Byrnes, Thomas J., 31, 32

Index • 151

cars, *42, 65, 132;* acquisition of, 42–43, 88, 92–95; Budd's proposal, 114; crane-car, *94,* 124, 125, *133;* described, *23,* 41–43; passenger-baggage combines, 60, 61; Peru in 2007, 125, *129;* reuse of, 120, *121,* 125, 132. *See also* appendix 1
catenary systems, 35–38, *40, 94*
Central New England RR, 17, 32
Chatham Four Corners, N.Y., 6
Choate, Charles F., Jr., 31, 73
citizens' actions. *See under* Westchester County
City & County Contract Co., 20, 27, 28, 80
Connecticut, plans for, 79–80, 81, 83–84
construction, NYW&B: catenary, *94;* earth work, 5, 35, *37, 54;* 1905–1906, *24,* 24–25; 1911, *30;* 1920–1930, 90–92, 95–97. *See also under* bridges; electrification
contractor payoff deals, 24
contractors, team track for, 68, 137
Cos Cob, Conn., 35, 38
County Transportation Co., 99–101, 135, 137
Coverdale & Colpitts, 112–13, 118

Danbury, Conn., 79–80, 84
Daniels, Winthrop, 111
demolition of NYW&B, 124
Depression era, 105–15; cost cutting, 113
Dohr, James L., 117–18, 124, 127
"Dyre Ave. shuttle," 125, *126*

Eastchester, N.Y., 12
Electric Railway Journal, 44, 69
electrification, 35–39; catenary systems, 35–38, *40, 94;* history of, 11. *See also* interlockings, NYW&B
elevated railways, 9, *10,* 11, *86. See also* Interborough Rapid Transit
Elliott, Howard, 72, 82
Engineering News editorial, 74
equipment, NYW&B, 43, *133;* list of (*see* appendix 1); shop facilities, 45–46. *See also* cars; *under* locomotives
expenses: construction, 24, 90; fixed, 88; rentals, 112–13; terminal fees, 75. *See also* tax bills

fares, NYW&B, 59–60, 99, 111, 114; collection of, 44–45, *49*
Fellheimer, Alfred, 33, 35, *47,* 141n5; interiors, *49;* shop complex, 45–46; station design, 43–44, *48, 50, 51, 52, 54*
finances, NYW&B: accounts, 87, 103, 106, 117; bankruptcy, 106–108, 110–15, 117; banks and, 25, 26–27; bondholder actions, 113–14, 118, 122–23; bonds, 28, 81, 88, 106, 123; capitalization, 32; investigations of, 72–74; profitability of buses, 101; receivership, 117–20, 122–24, 127; revenues, 87, 103, 117. *See also* expenses
Folk, Gov. Joseph, 28, 73
Freedman, Andrew, 20–21
freight business: NYW&B, *52,* 60–61, *67,* 68, 97, 137; WNRR, 80
freight yards, NYW&B, *62, 67, 109. See also* appendix 2

Garvin, Edwin L., 117–18
Gates, John W., 20
Gedney Farm Hotel, 61
Gilbert, Cass, 44, *55*
Golden Brothers, 68
Gotshall, William C., 19–20, 23–24, 28
Grand Central Terminal, 11, *64;* architects, 33; cost of, 74; 1870s, *4;* 1920s, 101, *102;* NYNH&H strategy and, 75–76, 89; usage fees, 75

Harlem River & Port Chester RR, 8–9
Harlem River terminal, NYW&B, 43, *63, 86, 89, 102,* 135; freight handling, 60–61; justifications for, 76; 1924 changes, 88–89, *89;* service to, 57–58
Harmon, Arthur L., 97
Harrison, N.Y., 12, 25, 92, *94*
Healy, Kent T., 74
Heathcote, Col. Caleb, 34–35, 44
Heathcote, N.Y., 97, *98;* buses to, 100; Donnybrook Lodge, 97, *98, 129;* freight house, *67;* station, 44, *52, 53, 129,* 137
Heathcote Land Corp., 97
Hill, James J., 14–17
Hincks, Judge Carroll C., 108, 112–13, 117
horsecars, 5, 7, 19
Housatonic RR, 84
Hudson & Manhattan Railroad, *23,* 41, 124
Hudson River Railroad, 6–7
Hunt, Samuel, 20
Hunt's Point, N.Y.: NYW&B service, 57–58, 60; station, *55,* 135
Hutchinson River Parkway, 105

Interborough Rapid Transit (IRT): cars, 1907, *10;* connections to, 61–68, 136, 137; "Dyre Ave. shuttle," 125, *126;* el terminals, 34, *63, 86,* 88; *World's Fair* cars, 86
interlockings, NYW&B, 39; NHRR-owned, 39, *41, 91;* operation precision, 58–59. *See*

also appendix 2; architecture: towers; junctions
Interstate Commerce Commission: on costs of NYW&B, 68; investigations, 27–28, 32, 72–74; labor ruling, 112
interurbans, 19

junctions: Columbus Ave., *56,* 58–59, *59, 67, 128;* Larchmont, 38, 90, *91, 92;* West Farms, *41, 121. See also* appendix 2

Knickerbocker Trust Co., 25, 26, 28
Knox, Judge John C., 117, 118–19, 124
Kreschollek, Fred, 58

labor relations, NYW&B, 61, 118, 120; wage-cut attempts, 112
LaGuardia, Fiorello, 122, 124, 125
Larchmont, N.Y., station, *110,* 136
Larchmont Gardens, 123, 136
Larchmont Manor, 100
Lawrence family, 71
legislation, public-rail, 122, 123, 124
Lehman, Gov. Herbert, 122, 123
Lipsett, Inc., 124
Lock Joint Pipe Co., 68
locomotives, NYW&B, 43, *67,* 68, 125, 132, *132, 133*
locomotives, steam: 1870s, *4;* 1880s, *7;* 1902, *10;* 1946, *121*

Mamaroneck, N.Y., 12; NYW&B service, 61, 90; station, *93,* 136; trolleys in, 99
Manhattan Railway, 9, 11
marketing, NYW&B, *22, 23,* 60–61, 101
McDonald, James P., 24
McLeod, A. A., 14
Mellen, Charles S., 14–17, *16, 70;* accusations vs., 71–72; blaming of, 72, 74; ICC testimony, 73, 75, 76; Morgan's trust in, 17; transactions by, 25–29, 31–32
"Metro-Urban," 101
Millbrook Co., 26, 28–29, 61; MtV&E and, 79; WNRR and, 81
Miller, George MacCulloch, 26, 32, 43
Miller, Leverett Saltonstall, 32–33, 106; annual statement, 87; on buses, 100; business plans, 98, 101–102; "Metro-Urban," 101; WNRR and, 79
Morgan, J. P., Jr. (Jack), 72
Morgan, J. Pierpont, 9, *15;* competitiveness of, 14, 17; death of, 72; historians' views of, 74–75; Mellen's idolatry of, 73; secret acquisitions, 26–29, 73

Morse, Charles W., 20
Moses, Robert, 120, 122
Mount Vernon, N.Y.: Columbus Ave. junction, *56,* 58–59, *59, 67, 128,* 136; Columbus Ave. viaduct, *30, 36, 107;* franchise, 57; NYW&B service, 57–58; population, 13; Willson's Woods Park, 84. *See also* Mount Vernon stations
Mount Vernon & Eastern RR, 79, 85
Mount Vernon stations, 136; East Sixth Street, 43, *53;* East Third Street, 43, 44, *48, 49;* freight terminals, 60–61, 68

National Register of Historic Places, *47,* 127
New England Navigational Co., 31
New England Transportation Co., 99
"New Haven RR." *See* New York, New Haven & Hartford RR
New Rochelle, N.Y., 12, 13, *115;* Larchmont junction, 38, 90, *91, 92,* 136; Mayor Harry Scott, 118; NYW&B service, 57–59; Wykagyl rock cut, *37. See also* New Rochelle stations
New Rochelle stations: North Ave., *45,* 136; Pine Brook, 90, *93,* 136; Quaker Ridge, 44, *54, 55, 66,* 125, 137; Wykagyl, *50,* 137
New York, Boston, Albany & Schenectady RR, 84–85
New York, Housatonic & Northern RR, 84, 85
New York, New Haven & Hartford RR, 7–8, *13,* 13–14, *15, 16, 17, 96;* bankruptcy, 106–108; buses, 99–101; cars shared, 92–95, 131–32, 134; Depression era, 106–108; financing of NYW&B, 32, 88, 108, 112–13; "Grand Central diversion," 75–76, 89; Harlem River branch, 8–9, *41,* 60, 65, *104, 121;* interlockings shared, 39, *41, 91;* lawsuits, 71–75; locomotives, *121;* NYBA&S and, 84–85; rentals to NYW&B, 110, 111, 112–14; secret deals, 25–29, 31–32; station relocations, 90, *94, 95;* stations shared, *55,* 90, *93, 94, 95, 110;* "suburban lines," 9; trolley systems, 17, 99, 100; WNRR and, 80–82. *See also* Charles S. Mellen; J. Pierpont Morgan
New York, Westchester & Boston RR: beginnings, 9, 13, 20, 32; costs of, 1, 68; innovations by, *23,* 40–42, 44–45, *49;* "last trip" events, 119; "New Haven RR" and, 1–2, 71–75; 1907 sale to NYNH&H, 25–27; 1939 restart attempts, 123–24; 1940 Bronx sale, 124; offices, *47;* overview, 1–2; routes (*see* routes, NYW&B); subsidiaries (*see* buses; Westchester Northern RR); terminal sharing, 90 (*see also* stations, NYNH&H).

See also business, NYW&B; cars; passenger service; stations, NYW&B
New York & Harlem RR, 4, 5–6, 7, 84
New York & New England RR, 8, 14, 84
New York & Port Chester RR, 19–20; merger with NYW&B, 32; 1906 construction, 25; route map, *18;* sale to "New Haven," 25–26, 28. *See also* William C. Gotshall
New York & Stamford Railway, 20, 99, 100, 135
New York & Westchester Townsite Co., 20
New York Central & Hudson River RR, 7, 10, 11–12, *12*. *See also* Cornelius Vanderbilt
New York Central RR, 6–7, *7,* 8, 11–12, *12, 13;* comparisons of, 34, 35, 59–60, 97, 103; locomotives, *7, 10;* Mellen and, 14; 1938 extra cars, 119; Putnam Division, 123; Reed & Stem, 33. *See also* Grand Central Terminal; New York & Harlem RR
New York City: acquiring NYW&B property, 120–22, 124–25; "elevateds," 9, *10,* 11; franchise, 24–25, 57; railroads in, 8–9, 11–12; steam prohibition in, 11; subway proposals, 101–103; terminals (*see* Bronx terminals); train overcrowding, 101–103; travel choices in, 61–64. *See also* Bronx, N.Y.; Grand Central Terminal; Interborough Rapid Transit; Port Authority of New York
New York City & Northern RR, 8
New York City & Westchester RR, 20
New York City Transit Commission, 101, 111
New York Edison, 38
New York Railroad & Development Co., 20
New York Railroad Commission, 20
New York State Public Service Commission, 33, 79, 119
Norris, Sen. George, 73
Northern Pacific RR, 14, 72

operating ratio, NYW&B, 87, 103, 117
operations, NYW&B, 35–39, 56, 57–59, *59. See also* interlockings, NYW&B; junctions; train lengths, NYW&B
overpasses. *See under* bridges

Palmer, Howard, 118
Panic of 1907, 26–27, 28
Parsons, Knapp, Brinckerhoff & Douglas, 102
Parsons, William Barclay, 20
passenger service: competition for, 61–68; cuts in the 1930s, 106; duplications by NHRR, 75–76; New York City problems, 101–103; numbers of riders, 99, 103, 106, 114, 119; reliability of, 58–59; schedules, 57–58, 106. *See also* buses: NYW&B; trolley systems

passengers, geographic distribution of, 99
Peckham Road Corp., 68
Pelham, N.Y., 12; earth fill, *37;* NYW&B station, 43–44, *51*
Pelham Parkway "subway," 35
Pelley, John J., 106
Perry, Marsden J., 25–28, 73, 79
Poor's Railroad Manual, 81
Port Authority of New York, 122, 123, 124
Port Chester, N.Y.: accidents in, 132; NYW&B service, 92, 99, 100; stations, 92, *96,* 123; trolleys in, 100
Port Chester branch: abandonment of, 118–19; construction of, 82, 89–92; 1938 damage to, 123; service, 58, 59; stations (*see* appendix 2; *under town names*)
power plants, 35, 38
Pratt, William A., 21
Prouty, Charles, 73

Railroad & Development Co., 24
railroads, N.Y., history, 5–12
real estate, Connecticut, 81
real estate development, 97; fraud in, 35; Gedney Farm, 61; rail lines' use in, 19. *See also* Heathcote, N.Y.
Reed, Charles, 33
Reed & Stem, 33, 141n5
right-of-way constructs, 35, *37*
Rockefeller, William, 26
routes, NYW&B: branches, 34, 89–92 (*see also* Port Chester branch; White Plains Branch, NYW&B); business analysis of, 58, 61–64; early plans, *21,* 21–22, *22,* 33–35; map ca. 1930, *x;* mileage of, 92; problems in, 75–76
Rye, N.Y.: NYW&B service, 92, 100; station, *95,* 137
Rye Beach, N.Y., 100–101

Sartorius, Irving A., 113–14, 122–23
Scarsdale, N.Y., 6, 12, 34–35, 99–100. *See also* Heathcote, N.Y.
Scarsdale Supply Co., 68, 97
schedules, NYW&B, 57–58, 106
Schramek, William E., 114
Scott, Mayor Harry, 118
scrapping operations, 124, 125
Second Avenue Railway, *10,* 19
sidings, NYW&B, 39, *45*
signals, NYW&B, 38–39
Skinner, William, 27
Smith, Charles H., 24
Soundview Transportation Co., 100, 101
Southern Westchester RR, 84
speeds of trains, 38–39, 59

Sprague, Frank J., 11
stations, NYNH&H: 1887–1888, *93, 94;* Harrison, *94;* Hunt's Point, *55;* Larchmont, *110;* Mamaroneck, *93;* Rye, *95*
stations, NYW&B, 43–45; baggage handling, 43, *52;* list of (*see* appendix 2); platforms, 44; surviving to 2007, *52, 93, 94,* 123, *127*. See also under town names
steel scrap, military, 124
Stetson, Francis Lynde, 26, 27, 74
Stillwell, Lewis B., *23,* 41–42
Suburban Rapid Transit Co., 9
"subway," Pelham Parkway, 35
subway proposals, Manhattan, 101–103

Tammany Democrats, 23, 28, 73
Tarrytown, N.Y., trolleys, 99
tax bills, 103, 108–10, 111–12, 118, 119
Technical World, 68
telephone system, NYW&B, 39
terminals, NYW&B. See stations, NYW&B
Third Avenue Ry., *86,* 100, 135, 136
Thorne, Oakleigh, 25–28, 73, 79
Throg's Neck, *21,* 33, 139n7
tickets. *See* fares, NYW&B
tracks, NYW&B: for contractors, 68; crossovers, 39; exclusive use, *60, 65, 120;* mainline, four-track, 34, *36, 39, 109;* structure of, 35; switching precision, 58–59, *59*
train lengths, NYW&B, 61, 88, *90,* 98–99, *111, 115*
trolley systems, 17, 99, 100; connections to NYW&B (*see* appendix 2)
trolleys, Rhode Island, 25
Tugwell, Rexford G., 122
tunnel, Mount Prospect, 5

U.S. Reconstruction Finance Corp., 106

Vanderbilt, Cornelius, 6–7; NYH&N and, 84
Vanderbilt, William K., 33

Warren, Whitney, 33
Weller, John, 24
Westchester County, 5, *7,* 12; architecture in, 43; Citizens Committee for Continuance, 114, 119; 1939 community actions, 124; Transit Commission, 101–102; trolleys in, 99. See also under town names
Westchester Electric RR, 136, 137
Westchester Northern RR, 79–83; route map, *78;* terminal, *82*
Westchester Street RR, *51,* 99, 100, 137
Westchester Street Transportation, 100
Western Railroad of Mass., 6
Westinghouse, George, 11
White Plains, N.Y., 6, 12; Bryant Ave. overpass, *38;* Gedney Farm Hotel, 61; NYH&N line to, 84; service to, 58–59, *59;* trolleys in, 99. See also White Plains stations
White Plains Branch, NYW&B: freight handling, 60–61, *62,* 68, *109;* justifications for, 76, 79–84; post-war years, 95–98; route, 34; start-up, 57; stations (see appendix 2; *under town names*)
White Plains stations: Gedney Way, 68, 95, 100, *118,* 137; Mamaroneck Ave., *51,* 137; Ridgeway, 95–97, 98, 137; Westchester Ave., 43, *62, 82, 112, 127,* 137
Wilgus, William, 33
Williams Bridge, N.Y., 6
Williamson, Pliny, 122

BOOKS IN THE RAILROADS PAST AND PRESENT SERIES

Landmarks on the Iron Railroad: Two Centuries of North American Railroad Engineering by William D. Middleton

South Shore: The Last Interurban (revised second edition) by William D. Middleton

"Yet there isn't a train I wouldn't take": Railroad Journeys by William D. Middleton

The Pennsylvania Railroad in Indiana by William J. Watt

In the Traces: Railroad Paintings of Ted Rose by Ted Rose

A Sampling of Penn Central: Southern Region on Display by Jerry Taylor

Katy Northwest: The Story of a Branch Line Railroad by Donovan L. Hofsommer

The Lake Shore Electric Railway by Herbert H. Harwood, Jr., and Robert S. Korach

The Pennsylvania Railroad at Bay: William Riley McKeen and the Terre Haute and Indianapolis Railroad by Richard T. Wallis

The Bridge at Quebec by William D. Middleton

History of the J. G. Brill Company by Debra Brill

When the Steam Railroads Electrified by William D. Middleton

Uncle Sam's Locomotives: The USRA and the Nation's Railroads by Eugene L. Huddleston

Metropolitan Railways: Rapid Transit in America by William D. Middleton

Limiteds, Locals, and Expresses in Indiana, 1838–1971 by Craig Sanders

Perfecting the American Steam Locomotive by J. Parker Lamb

Invisible Giants: The Empires of Cleveland's Van Sweringen Brothers by Herbert H. Harwood, Jr.

From Small Town to Downtown: A History of the Jewett Car Company, 1893–1919 by Lawrence A. Brough and James H. Graebner

Steel Trails of Hawkeyeland: Iowa's Railroad Experience by Don L. Hofsommer

Still Standing: A Century of Urban Train Station Design by Christopher Brown

The Indiana Rail Road Company: America's New Regional Railroad by Christopher Rund

Amtrak in the Heartland by Craig Sanders

The Men Who Loved Trains: The Story of Men Who Battled Greed to Save an Ailing Industry by Rush Loving Jr.

The Train Of Tomorrow by Ric Morgan

Evolution of the American Diesel Locomotive by J. Parker Lamb

The Encyclopedia of North American Railroads edited by William D. Middleton, George M. Smerk, and Roberta L. Diehl

Herbert H. Harwood, Jr., has concurrently been a railroad historian, writer, photographer, and working railroader. A history graduate of Princeton University, he received his MBA from Columbia University and then spent 30 years in various management positions at the Chesapeake & Ohio and Baltimore & Ohio and their successor, CSX Transportation. He has written 12 books on railroad and electric railway history.